"What is more relevant today than to point
weapon against *all* kinds of unrighteousness,
ism is Father's Book, the Holy Bible? Yes, in
is still there (but still not everywhere as Loren points out), but the
need today is for teachers, followers, disciples, pioneers, reformers
(and what about the occasional "smuggler"?) to penetrate *every*
stronghold of unbelief and there boldly proclaim the Lordship of
Christ. The world is waiting, the doors are open, God is waiting—
if you still are, then read this book. It's not about problems, but
about solutions. Wish I had written it."
Brother Andrew, "God's Smuggler"

"I believe that *The Book That Transforms Nations* is one of the most
significant books ever written on missions. I know of no other book
like this one. It is a rare and exceptional book that brings to bear
a wholistic view of the Kingdom of God with historical examples
and models of where it's been done right up to our own time in history.... I will require all of our church planters and interns to digest
this book. It took Loren a lifetime to understand these things—
may we practice them in all our lives! This could be the most significant contribution Loren has made thus far to see the Great
Commission completed."
*Bob Roberts, Senior Pastor, NorthWood Church; Founder, Glocalnet;
Author,* Transformation and Glocalization

"*The Book That Transforms Nations* instructs, informs, and inspires
servants of God worldwide in how God moves in transforming
nations. His Word releases power to change any nation. Loren
Cunningham can speak authoritatively on the topic, first because
he received the vision of transforming nations more than thirty
years ago; second, because he founded what became the largest
non-formal educational school in the world where the Bible is
taught faithfully; and third, because he is most likely the only missionary who has traveled to every nation on earth."
Luis Bush, Transform World Connections, International Facilitator

(continued on next page)

"It is inspiring to read about the difference God's Word has made in the past. It leads us to imagine what difference it will make in the future if we will just apply it to life and culture."
Steve Douglass, President of Campus Crusade for Christ International

"In these refreshing pages, Loren Cunningham shows again that when the truths of the Bible are put into practice, transformation is the result—for an individual, a family, or a nation. Loren demonstrates from the pages of history that those who delight themselves in the Law of the Lord will be fruitful and prosper."
Paul Eshleman, Founder, The JESUS Film Project

"In the global village, our future depends on the future of all nations...and the future of each nation depends on its ability to receive God's word. In this book Loren Cunningham presents his insightful and visionary answer to the question: how do different cultures come to obey God and listen to Jesus Christ? It is fascinating to follow him in his exploration of so many different people and cultures through history and geography."
Prof. Dr. John C. Badoux, Honorary President of the Swiss Federal Institute of Technology Lausanne (EPFL)

"In *The Book That Transforms Nations*, Loren sets the foundation for why the Word of God is not only God's instrument in drawing people to Christ in salvation but also an instrument in transforming whole peoples.... I believe this book will not only help to disciple its readers but also honor God's Word and exalt it to its proper place. 'For you have exalted above all things your name and your word' (Ps. 138:2)."
Danny Lehmann, Director of YWAM in the Hawaiian Islands and member of YWAM's International Global Leadership Team

"*The Book That Transforms Nations* is both a reminder of what God has done in the past as well as practical in what every believer can do. Loren Cunningham will ignite your imagination and renew hope in you for the world."
Rick Warren, author, The Purpose Driven Life

"In the many years I have known closely this modern missionary statesman, Loren Cunningham has not only had a passion for the lost, but a drive from the Holy Spirit to see the Bible distributed, studied, and taught. As I read this book, I saw why the compulsion has always been there. God's Word really does form history."

Dean Sherman, International Dean, College of Christian Ministries, University of the Nations

"God's living Word allows us to meet our Lord Jesus Christ. We can then receive the Holy Spirit's power to transform ourselves, our families, our society, and our nation. In Korea, we received the Bible and were filled with the Holy Spirit. The great revival and transformation in the twentieth century became legendary. This transformation is still going on, not only in Korea but also abroad. Loren Cunningham's new book vividly shows people everywhere how to take the precious first steps to change their countries. We must read this book!"

Dr. KunMo Chung, Chairman, Korean National Prayer Breakfast; Chairman, Habitat for Humanity Korea; President, Myongji University

"God's love for all the nations of the earth is conveyed through Loren's intriguing factual accounts and real-life stories. In the face of seemingly ever-increasing spiritual darkness worldwide, this book provides hope and a reminder of the power of the Bible."

Joyce Meyer, best-selling author and Bible teacher

"Loren Cunningham is unquestionably one of the twentieth century's greatest missionary leaders and continues into the twenty-first as one of the Church's foremost missionary statesmen. It is no surprise that a book on *The* Book and its power to transform cultures would be written by a man who is a lifelong evidence of Christ, the Living Word, being manifestly incarnate in one of His faithful servants."

Jack W. Hayford, President, International Foursquare Churches; Chancellor, The King's College and Seminary

THE POWER OF THE **BIBLE** TO CHANGE ANY COUNTRY

Other Books by Loren Cunningham

Daring to Live on the Edge:
The Adventure of Faith and Finances

Is That Really You, God?
Hearing the Voice of God

Making Jesus Lord:
The Dynamic Power of Laying Down Your Rights

Why Not Women?
A Fresh Look at Scripture on Women
in Missions, Ministry, and Leadership

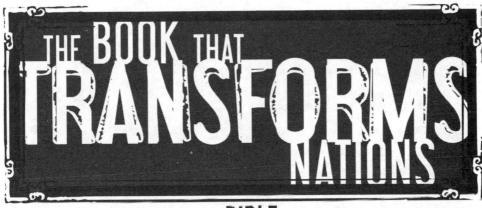

THE POWER OF THE **BIBLE** TO CHANGE ANY COUNTRY

Loren Cunningham
with Janice Rogers

P.O. BOX 55787   SEATTLE, WA 98155

YWAM Publishing is the publishing ministry of Youth With A Mission. Youth With A Mission (YWAM) is an international missionary organization of Christians from many denominations dedicated to presenting Jesus Christ to this generation. To this end, YWAM has focused its efforts in three main areas: (1) training and equipping believers for their part in fulfilling the Great Commission (Matthew 28:19), (2) personal evangelism, and (3) mercy ministry (medical and relief work).

For a free catalog of books and materials, contact:

YWAM Publishing
P.O. Box 55787, Seattle, WA 98155
(425) 771-1153 or (800) 922-2143
www.ywampublishing.com

The Book That Transforms Nations:
The Power of the Bible to Change Any Country
Copyright © 2007 by Loren Cunningham

13 12 11 10 09 08   10 9 8 7 6 5 4 3 2

Published by YWAM Publishing
P.O. Box 55787, Seattle, WA 98155

ISBN-10: 1-57658-381-3; ISBN-13: 978-1-57658-381-4

Library of Congress Cataloging-in-Publication Data
Cunningham, Loren.
   The book that transforms nations : the power of the Bible to change any country /
Loren Cunningham with Janice Rogers.
      p. cm.
   ISBN-13: 978-1-57658-381-4 (pbk.)
   ISBN-10: 1-57658-381-3 (pbk.)
   1. Sociology, Biblical. I. Rogers, Janice. II. Title.
   BS670.C76 2006
   270—dc22   2005034278

Unless otherwise noted, Scripture quotations in this book are taken from the Holy Bible, New International Version®, Copyright © 1973, 1978, 1984 by the International Bible Society. Used by permission of Zondervan Publishing House. Verses marked KJV are taken from the King James Version of the Bible. Verses marked NASB are taken from the New American Standard Bible, © 1960, 1962, 1963, 1968, 1971, 1972, 1973, 1975, 1977 by The Lockman Foundation. Used by permission. Verses marked NLT are taken from the Holy Bible, New Living Translation, copyright © 1996. Used by permission of Tyndale House Publishers, Inc., Wheaton, IL 60189. All rights reserved.

Printed in the United States of America.

I dedicate this book to Darlene…a loving wife, a great mother, and a true partner. I cannot imagine my life without you.

Acknowledgments

We wish to thank those who gave their time and expertise to make this book a reality. First, a great big thank you to Pacheco Pyle, who poured herself into creating the first draft and spent countless hours in research. Thank you to Marit Newton and Warren Walsh and others at YWAM Publishing for going above and beyond the call to duty. We're also grateful to others who helped with stories and facts and made the manuscript readable, including Peter Adams, Larry Allen, Paul Allen, Al Akimoff, the Rev. Dr. E. H. Jim Ammerman, Tom Bloomer, Gail Boemker, Terry Bragg, Ryan Davis, Carol Dowsett, Bill Efinger, Katherine Ewing, Herbert Ford, George Foster, Jeff Fountain, Dawn Gauslin, Lynn Green, Phyllis Griswold, Thomas Grunder, Keith and Marilynn Hamilton, Debbie Hicks, Olivia Jackson, Todd Johnson, Warren and Gayle Keapproth, Emele Kila, YoungSook Luce, April Otis McCallum, Alv Magnus, Vishal and Ruth Mangalwadi, Colleen Milstein, Bob Moffitt, Kalafi Moala, Oliver Olson, Lisa Orvis, Colin Pettit, Winkie Pratney, Pari and Diane Ricard, Bráulia Ribeiro, Ricardo Rodrigues, Jeff Rogers, Jim Rogers, Ed Sherman, Debbi Smith, Ronald Smith, Jim Stier, and Tom Wheaton.

Contents

Preface

As I write this book, I need to admit up front that I don't consider myself a scholar. I have several degrees, including both undergraduate and graduate degrees from the University of Southern California, so I am not an uneducated man. But I know people who have devoted themselves to research and study in a way that I stand in awe of. These experts include godly men and women who have studied specific issues or nations in-depth, combining their expertise with a devotion to the Word of God.

However, I do have a unique vantage point as I talk about nations and the issues facing them. From my first call to ministry at the age of thirteen, I've been interested in the whole world. As an adult, I have traveled continually, often going to thirty or forty countries each year. I have visited every country on earth—a rare privilege shared with perhaps only a dozen other people. While doing so I have been able to observe nations as they change. This book draws on my lifetime of observing that process and a lifelong pursuit of hearing God's Word for the nations. My vantage point has not been in-depth—it's more like a mile wide and an inch deep. I can offer the broad strokes—the big picture, if you will. In many chapters of this book we only touch on areas that deserve much deeper treatment. I hope this book will open the discussion. I trust it will whet your appetite for further study into how some nations have emerged and others have remained in despair.

I truly believe we *can* change the world for the better. God has given us keys to every problem we face in the twenty-first century—problems in developed countries and developing ones alike. Everything, everywhere can be changed.

I have devoted my life to that purpose. Along the way I have had the honor of working with millions of young men and women sharing the same goal. I wrote this book with the prayer that you, too, will join this effort. The body of Christ has the answers to the world's greatest problems. We hold the answers between the covers of a Book many of us have known all our lives. We can see nations changed. As we sow the Bible into more and more lives, we will see the worldviews of people and nations realigned. That will transform their thinking, their values, and their behavior.

As you read this book, look for the basic ideas of the Bible that will renew nations. Also look for methods, especially storytelling. God himself started with a story in Genesis, and 70 percent of the Bible is narrative. Stories wrap truth in emotional context; that's what makes the impact. God's stories are eternal, while ours show how the truth is relevant today. May the upcoming stories of nation changers spur you on to use the Bible to transform nations.

Part 1

We Can Win It All
or Lose It All

Chapter 1

Losing and Finding
The Book

Many years ago in the foothills of the eastern Himalayas, a missionary was preaching. As he stood in a dusty village marketplace, he held up his Bible and said, "This is God's Book!" Then he told the people what was in it.

After he spoke, the crowd scattered. A man then approached him, layered in the handwoven robes of a village high in the Himalayas. He asked the missionary, "Is that really God's Book?"

"Yes, this is God's Book. It's for every area of life."

The villager said, "May I tell you the story of my tribe?" He began to tell the story that had been passed down from his father, his father's father, and his father before him. Their tribe had come from lands far west of the great mountains. "We always lived by God's Book. But our ancestors were driven from their lands." He went on to tell how they had made the perilous journey east, over the mountains. "While making the crossing, our people were caught in a storm and they lost The Book."

Now his tribe didn't know how to live. They had been looking for The Book for many generations.

"Two weeks ago an old woman in our tribe had a dream," he said. She dreamed of a foreigner standing in this particular village, holding up The Book. If the elders sent someone on this day, he would find the foreigner. "They sent me," he finished. "Will you bring God's Book to my tribe so that we will know how to live again?"

A missionary to the Himalayas shared this remarkable experience in my dad's church when I was a teenager. Now, many years later, I can't remember the missionary's name, but I've never forgotten his story. As he spoke, I pictured those people trekking across the Himalayas. I could see them straining against the stinging wind, blinded by the snow. I imagined their joy as they found a safe valley, then their frustration and pain when they realized they had lost their only copy of Scripture. How tragic.

Sadly, the tragedy of losing God's Book and forgetting how to live has occurred among people throughout history.

Descent into Madness

The Bible tells of another people who lost The Book and plunged into darkness. During the reign of King Manasseh, the kingdom of Judah turned from the living God.[1] The people rapidly defiled the land with sorcery and witchcraft. They filled the countryside and even the Lord's temple with pagan altars, graven images, and Asherah poles. They consulted mediums and spiritists instead of seeking God. King Manasseh set up idol worship inside God's temple,[2] and male prostitutes served their patrons' appetites there.[3] The people even worshiped the idol Molech by heating its stone image until it was red hot, then placing their newborn babies on it to burn to death.[4] The king also burned his sons as offerings to Molech.[5] In fact, King Manasseh "shed so much innocent blood that he filled Jerusalem from end to end."[6]

When Manasseh's son Amon became king, he was so wicked that his own officials assassinated him two years after he rose to power.[7] Then the people sought revenge and massacred those who had plotted against Amon. In the midst of all this bloodshed, an eight-year-old boy, Josiah, was put on his father's throne. Can you imagine a more precarious situation than what this boy faced?

Amazingly, in this atmosphere of conspiracies, betrayal, and danger, the young king didn't fall back on his father's evil ways.[8] Instead, Josiah began to seek God.

Unearthing a Long-Lost Treasure

When he was twenty-six years old, Josiah ordered the rebuilding of God's temple. One day in the midst of the rubble and dust of this great restoration project, Hilkiah the priest found something wrapped in hides. As he removed the protective layer, he saw carefully marked yellowing sheets. His heart skipped a beat as he realized what he held: long-forgotten scrolls, the Word of God— abandoned by the people, then lost entirely.

The priest hurried to Shaphan the secretary, cradling the ancient manuscripts in his arms. "I have found the Book!" Hilkiah cried.[9]

Shaphan brought the crumbling parchments directly to King Josiah, announcing what Hilkiah the priest had found. At the king's command, Shaphan began to read the Scriptures aloud. As Josiah listened, he felt his heart pierced with guilt over his sins and those of his people. He cried out in repentance, begging God to forgive him and the people. He promised to obey the Lord in every way, just as it was spelled out in those scrolls. Then Josiah brought all the people together, "from the least to the greatest," and read God's entire Word aloud to them.[10]

A great revival and transformation began, reshaping the whole country. The people learned about God's Covenant in The Book and the blessings that would follow if they entered into such a contract with God. They learned what straying had cost them. The pain of this realization hit them, and they followed their king in repentance, weeping and begging God to forgive them and heal their country.

Josiah then led the people to get rid of the evil in their country. At the king's command, they destroyed pagan shrines and stopped their vile practices, driving out the prostitutes from the temple and obliterating the places where they had killed their babies. Josiah ordered the people to shatter all the idols, Asherah poles, and graven images, to burn them and scatter the ashes.[11]

In every way, Josiah turned his heart to obey the words of Scripture and guided his people to do the same.[12] Unfortunately, the kings who followed Josiah again led the people away from The Book, and they again fell on hard times. But we can learn from King Josiah and his people how to bring healing and restoration to our countries today.

The Book That Transforms Nations

Whether in ancient Israel, the distant Himalayas, or our own nation, there are many ways to lose God's Word. The results are always tragic. But blessings always come when a nation finds God's Book again. Throughout history, the record is clear: *when a critical mass of people have the Bible and apply what it teaches in their lives, a nation is transformed.* That's the big idea behind this book—one that we will explore in detail.

A Two-Edged Sword

It's wonderful to learn there's hope for our nations if they embrace the Bible and put its truths into practice. However, before we get warm, fuzzy thoughts about how great it is to have the Bible, we need to seriously consider the other side of this premise, because the opposite is also true, right now in whatever nation we're in: *whenever a critical number of people abandon the Bible and stop applying it in their personal lives, that nation begins to destroy itself.*

The blessings we enjoy because of the Bible are not a permanent heritage. Our choices determine whether we hold on to them or not. Many believers are at least somewhat aware of our biblical foundations in Western civilization. Most don't know how close we are to losing the blessings those foundations provide.

We need to ask ourselves some hard questions. Have we gone past a point of no return in the "de-Christianizing" of the West? Are we about to lose our leadership and the way of life we have come to expect? If we reject the source of our blessings, how long can we continue to enjoy liberty, security, creativity, and material prosperity? I believe there are reasons for concern and reasons for hope, which we will see in the next chapter.

Chapter 2

What Will It Take?

China is rapidly becoming the leader of the world, while the West threatens to spiral into decline.

This fact hit me afresh during a conversation with a reporter from China. We were among thousands gathered from many nations to Gisborne, New Zealand, at the literal dawning of a new millennium. Many members of the international media were among the crowds lining Gisborne beaches in the predawn darkness that day, because the world's day begins in this first city bordering the international date line. And that of course made it the first city to see the sunrise of the new millennium. I had gone there to speak at a gathering of believers welcoming the year 2000 in praise and worship.

During this historic moment I struck up a conversation with a reporter from one of China's main newspapers. "China can become the new world leader in this century," I told him. The man looked at me in amazement. I continued, "China will become the new world leader within the next three or four generations if two conditions are met..."

After I told the reporter the two conditions, he stood there looking thoughtful and a bit hopeful. I, on the other hand, was sobered as I realized what a precarious position my own country was in.

What are the two conditions that must be met for China to become the world's number one leader?

The first condition: China will become the world's superpower if its people continue to become followers of Jesus at the present rate, founding their lives on the Bible.

A Stunning Growth

To see what's happening in China, we need to understand some of the background. For decades now, communist teaching has radically diminished China's traditional religions, Taoism and Buddhism. This is especially true among the nation's leaders and change agents. The resulting vacuum has given way to a stunning growth of the Christian church, for despite years of effort on the part of the communists, the Chinese refuse to believe there is no spiritual dimension to life. The undocumented house churches—the so-called underground church—are the fastest growing in the world. Experts say the Chinese church is growing at a stunning 3 percent to 4 percent per year,[1] bringing the estimated total to more than 110 million, or 8.5 percent of the population.[2]

It's hard to comprehend numbers like that. But think of it! If these believers were a country, they would be the eleventh largest nation in the world.[3]

The Word of God is quickly taking root in the lives of the Chinese people. Interestingly, many of these new converts are young people, taught all their lives that there is no God. Despite persecution that ranges from loss of job opportunities to loss of freedom and even loss of their lives, millions of Chinese are turning to Christ. They are finding God and his Book. According to David Aikman, former Beijing Bureau Chief for *Time* and longtime China observer, "China is becoming a Christian nation. I expect China to be 20 to 30 percent Christian in the next twenty years."[4]

A Secret Seminary Graduation

I recently saw some of this growth firsthand as I gathered with believers in the back room of an old factory in the suburb of a major Chinese city. Black plastic covered all the windows. Friends with cell phones were posted on all the roads leading to our meeting place to warn us if the police came. Even with all these precautions, the danger was so great that the people sang their hymns in hushed tones.

I had come to preach to the graduating class of a secret seminary in China. I was humbled to be their commencement speaker. Most of these young people had faced persecution. Some had been imprisoned. Twelve of their alumni have already become martyrs. Yet as I listened to their muffled but fervent worship, I caught their excitement. They were undaunted, courageous, ready to pursue their ministries at any cost.

The young men and women I saw that day are a tiny part of a movement that is amazing church historians and striking fear in the hearts of some of China's leaders.[5] If the Chinese continue to place their hope in the God of the Bible and continue to obey his Word, their nation will prosper—and may soon lead the world.

The second condition for China to become the leader of the world will be fulfilled if Western nations continue to turn away from the Bible at the present rate. America and other Western nations are faltering in their leadership.

"Is America an Undeveloped Country?"

That was the question economist Dr. Michael Schluter, coauthor of *The R Factor*, asked a group of YWAM leaders recently. Dr. Schluter, founder of the Relationships Foundation, was a key player in South Africa's reconciliation efforts after the end of apartheid.

When Dr. Schluter raised this surprising question, we were a bit taken aback. He went on to explain that perhaps God judges a nation not by its income but by how well it obeys Scripture—particularly God's great commandments to love him and to love one another.[6] If healthy relationships were the standard by which a nation is rated rather than average income or gross domestic product, the United States would have a far different rating than it has.

Let's look at the facts. America has one of the highest divorce rates in the world—43 percent of first marriages end in separation or divorce within fifteen years.[7] America holds more than two million inmates in prison—the highest per capita in the world.[8] And addiction to alcohol, drugs, gambling, and pornography are running rampant.[9]

Why is American society so broken when more than 84 percent of Americans identify themselves as Christian?[10] The answer is clear. While many say they're born again, and nearly 70 percent[11] go to church every week, they are not living their lives according to God's Word. According to a 2002 poll by the Barna Group of Ventura, California, only 7 percent of adults ages eighteen to thirty-five make moral choices based on the Bible; for older people, those over thirty-five, the percentage is somewhat higher—18 percent.[12]

What are Americans relying on to make their choices? According to this poll, most make decisions based on "feelings" or "beneficial outcomes" for themselves.[13]

Europe Abandons Its Inheritance

The nations of Western Europe are turning away from God and the Bible even more quickly than America is. Europeans increasingly view the church and belief in God as outdated, irrelevant, and an impediment to progress. The long-term, large-scale European Values Study shows how far Europeans have departed from their Christian heritage.[14] Only 21 percent of Europeans say religion is "very important" to them, and just 15 percent attend a place of worship once a week.[15] Few believe in things like heaven, hell, or sin.[16]

Other research adds to this depressing picture. In England, only 11 percent attend church as often as once a month.[17] No wonder U.K. rates for divorce, illegitimacy, suicide, and drug abuse are so high, with increasing violence in the cities.[18] In Norway, half the children are born to unmarried mothers, and it's increasingly common for couples not to get married at all.[19] In Germany, the birthplace of the Reformation, only 8 percent go to church regularly.[20]

Sadly, across these once-Christian nations, there is often hostility to anything even remotely related to the church.[21] Instead, New Age, pagan, and occult philosophies are growing increasingly popular and mainstream.[22]

The rise of Islam in Europe adds to all this. Muslim births far outnumber non-Muslim. For reasons experts still don't understand, Europeans are having fewer babies. They have a negative birthrate—not enough to replace themselves.[23] On the other hand, Europe has brought in millions of guest workers, mostly from the Middle East and North Africa. The Muslim immigrants have high birthrates.[24] If this trend continues, Islam will be the predominant religion in Europe by the end of this century.

While Western nations fear the increase of Islam in Europe, they seem blind to a greater problem—the loss of their own faith. If we in the West continue to deny God's relevance, or even his existence, and especially if we continue to turn away from absolute truths revealed in the Bible, our leadership will decline. Our cultures will turn more and more to pleasure seeking, materialism, irresponsibility, dishonesty, corruption, and violence. We will descend into poverty. Like Judah during the reign of King Manasseh, America and the West will crumble. And if China continues its phenomenal church growth, it will become the new world leader within three or four generations.

However, I do not believe the West has to decline. We can see both China and the West—and all the nations of the world—rise to the potential God has instilled in every land. We can even see the West and China living in peace and unity, serving the same God. We can see our countries turned around; we can see our foundations restored. And those foundations rest in one book—God's Book.

When we place our hope in God and by the power of the Holy Spirit begin to disciple the nations, teaching them all he has revealed in his Book, we can see every nation changed. Do we dare to believe and act?

Chapter 3

We Can Turn the Tide

Is it possible to transform a community, a city, a country? Jesus must have thought so. He told us to pray that his kingdom would come and that his will would be done on earth as it is in heaven.[1] He told us to disciple all nations and teach them to do all that he has commanded us.[2]

If it weren't possible for God's will to be done on earth and for nations to learn from God's wise commandments, would Jesus have given us these charges? No. He is just and loving. He wouldn't ask us to do something if it weren't possible for us to do it. Clearly, he didn't intend for us to sit back and accept the status quo.

Some people claim we cannot limit evil on earth. They say the times are supposed to get worse and worse until the Lord returns. While I agree that evil is certainly increasing, Jesus was not a fatalist, and neither am I. We can see our countries transformed. The Bible says that where sin increases, grace increases even more.[3] The Lord does not want us to give up in the face of mounting evil.

Do you believe the future can be better? Notice that Jesus' command to disciple and teach all nations comes right between two very good reasons for hope: he declares that he has all authority, and he promises to be with us. Jesus says,

> All authority in heaven and on earth has been given to me. *Therefore* go and make disciples of all nations, baptizing them in the name of the Father and of the Son and of the Holy Spirit, and teaching them to obey everything I have commanded you. And *surely I am with you always,* to the very end of the age. (Matt. 28:18–20, author's italics)

He doesn't leave us alone to turn the nations around. He doesn't expect us to do it in our own power. The Alpha and Omega invites us to work with *him* under *his* authority.

When we read the Bible, we gain confidence. We find out God created everything and is holding it all together—what we see and what we can't see.[4] Jesus isn't sitting back at ease, unconcerned about the state of our world. He is active, using his power and authority to reconcile nations and people to him.[5] And he is asking us to join him in this, the greatest struggle in history.[6]

Living in Reality

If we give in to despair or apathy, we aren't living according to reality. We need to look at who we are in Christ and get some strength in our backbone.

I've asked many congregations around the world, "How many of you have been saved?" Hands go up all over the auditoriums. Then I ask, "How many of you are perfect?" No one raises a hand. Then I ask, "How many are a whole lot better than you were before you were born again?" All of their hands go up.

We can see God transform nations the way we've seen him transform our lives. The apostle John said, "The one who is in you is greater than the one who is in the world."[7] The apostle Paul said Christ is over *every* power and authority.[8] When we look at the world in light of these truths, we should realize that sin and brokenness don't have to triumph. We should stand up and do everything we can to see that they don't.

The World Doesn't Have to Be This Evil

Some might say I'm being unrealistic, that I'm promoting some kind of utopia. No. There's no perfect nation until Jesus returns and establishes the New Jerusalem. But the world doesn't have to be this evil either. Sin is getting darker, but the light is getting brighter too. The Bible says the darkness will never extinguish the light.[9] Jesus said he's the light of the world, and he also said that we, his followers, are the light of the world.[10]

An Island Filled with Believers

I'm encouraged when I visit places where people of the light outnumber those of darkness. The island of Atafu in the Tokelau group is one of these places. I came there aboard one of YWAM's Marine Reach ships.[11] We were visiting a number of nations in the mid-Pacific, doing evangelism with simple puppet shows, teaching the people, and offering medical help. When we came to Atafu, we found that virtually everyone on this island of 275 people had committed his or her life to Jesus. When the people learned we were believers too, they welcomed us instantly and warmly. We set up our puppet show in the open marketplace and soon drew a crowd. As our team moved the puppets, acting out a lighthearted gospel message, I looked around me. The adults were laughing freely, just like the children. I sighed and took it all in. What a wonderful, stress-free environment!

Later, the pastor of the island's only church came to me privately and shared his concerns. He was worried because one of the men was fermenting coconut juice into alcohol and getting drunk occasionally. The pastor also told me that some of the people lied sometimes. I encouraged him, but thought to myself about what pastors are facing in other parts of the world. How wonderful that these were Atafu's biggest problems.

The contrast couldn't have been greater when we went to the next island in the chain, traveling overnight on our ship to get there. We soon discovered that this neighboring island was Christian in name only. Although they welcomed us politely, we could sense that the islanders didn't really want us there. They were stiff and ill at ease and seemed to be simmering with resentment. With sadness we learned that there had just been a rape on the island— something unheard of on nearby Atafu.

Of Bowls and Beds

How can we see the light shine in our communities the way it does on the island of Atafu? How can we see light overcoming darkness more and more throughout the world? It will happen only when we become fully engaged. Jesus said we are the light of the world, but we can't be passive about it. In Mark 4:21, he used the examples of lighting a lamp and putting it under a bowl or putting it under a bed. What was he saying?

A bowl symbolizes material provision. If all we're living for is to meet our needs and the needs of our family, we are putting our light under a bowl. We're living for materialism and not letting our light shine.

Jesus also said not to put our lamp under a bed. The bed is a symbol for ease. If all we're living for is to be comfortable, to avoid ever getting into any situation where we are ill at ease, then we are hiding the light of Christ.

The Lord wants his light to shine in all the world so that even those living in areas of great darkness will see it.[12] This will happen only when we start obeying him, asking him how to take his light to the world. What does Jesus himself tell us?

Not Only Salvation but Discipleship

If we want to transform nations, we must first lead people to receive Jesus Christ as their personal Savior. Jesus told us in Mark 16:15 to go into the whole world and preach the good news to everyone. That's the starting point. And yet more than one and a half billion people are still waiting for us to obey that command- ment. To put it another way, one-fourth of the world has never heard the gospel.[13] We've got to take the light out there. As we give people the chance to respond to the good news, they are trans- ferred out of what Paul calls the dominion of darkness into the kingdom of light.[14] That's what it means to be saved. It's a change of citizenship.

But even if we lead people to do this—giving every person on earth the chance to respond to the gospel—that is not enough. Salvation is only half of the Great Commission. Jesus gave us the other half—discipleship—in Matthew 28:19–20. There he told us we were to make disciples, and not just of individuals (as emphasized in Mark 16:15). In Matthew 28, he tells us to think in terms of entire nations.

Let's look again at Jesus' words from Matthew 28:19–20.

Make Disciples

Go and make disciples...

What does it mean to make disciples? Discipleship is the process of leading a person to transformation according to the standards of the Bible. Paul said in Romans 12:2 that transformation is getting a new mind—a new way of thinking. Transformed thinking comes as a person submits to God, listening to him and taking in his Word.

We disciple others by following Jesus' methods—a classic model for all teachers. First, Jesus did things in front of his disciples. Then he taught them the meaning of what he had done. Next he gave his disciples the opportunity to try it out for themselves, coaching them as they copied his behavior. After that he sent them out to do it on their own. Then they came back and reported their results.[15] That is the process of discipleship.

In the coming chapters we're going to see many examples of how we get from discipling individuals to discipling nations. In short, we disciple nations by starting with individuals, just as Jesus did. As we see individuals transformed, applying God's truth to all areas of their lives and in whatever area of society they live and work in, they will affect others, who will, in turn, affect still others. At some point there will be enough—a minority but a powerful one—to change the whole country. Jesus used the example of yeast to explain this process—a small lump affects the entire mass.[16] It becomes viral.

All Nations

Make disciples of all nations...

Jesus charged us to make disciples of *all* nations. All. No exceptions. He didn't say to go to the easy places or where it was legal to make converts. He told us to go to all. We're not to avoid any country because it is too hard, too large, too dangerous, too hopeless, too familiar or too "foreign," too far or too near. The gospel and its accompanying blessings are for all nations. John Wesley once said, "I look upon all the world as my parish."[17] We need to enlarge our thinking to include the whole earth, to see it as God sees it—with every human being and every country precious to him.

Baptize Them

Baptizing them in the name of the Father and of the Son and of the Holy Spirit...

Later in this book we'll see the importance of God in three persons when it comes to discipling nations. But what about Jesus' command to baptize? Some may ask, *How can you baptize a nation?* Of course you can't literally baptize a nation the way you can an individual. So what does Jesus mean here? As we baptize more and more individuals, introducing them to the Word and to Jesus, the Living Word, we will eventually have a believing minority that will change their country. That is the way entire nations can be immersed in and resurrected to a biblical worldview, with changes in every part of their societies.

Teach Them

Teaching them to obey everything I have commanded you...

Jesus also told us to *teach* all nations, and he gave us our curriculum—*everything* he has taught us. That's our curriculum—everything. The whole Bible is our textbook for teaching the nations. Notice that it's not just head knowledge we're to emphasize either. Jesus said to teach the nations to *obey*.

This is a huge job, but it's not beyond our reach. We can do anything and everything Jesus asks of us, as long as he gives us strength.[18]

Jesus himself lived out the whole Word for us. He came to earth to show us what the truth looks like in real life. Then he told us to go teach others, promising that he will be with us. He even summarized the message we are to deliver. He said that the most important commandments were to love the Lord our God with all our heart and with all our soul and with all our mind, and to love our neighbor as ourselves.[19] That's our message in a nutshell, the principles we're to teach the nations.

However, cold, impersonal principles, no matter how good they are, will never change people or nations. We spread the kingdom of God when we make a covenant with God to live by his principles. We forsake all rebellion against him and receive his forgiveness through faith in his Son. We come alive. His Spirit can then fill us and make his Word a living thing. We begin to discover who the Living Word within the written Word is. Jesus works to make his principles part of our character. Our character, expressed through our words and actions, becomes the yeast in our society, wherever we are, influencing it for righteousness. This is the way God's kingdom comes and his will is done on earth as it is in heaven.

Chapter 4

Revival or
Transformation?

We hear much these days about the need for revival in our time. But revival is not enough. Our nations need *transformation*. What is the difference?

In revival, many people come to experience the power of God. Thousands come to know Jesus as their Savior, sometimes a majority in a community. People abandon sinful pursuits, and often there are expressions of the supernatural power of God, with the sick healed and other miraculous signs. It's a time of great excitement, a time when people can hardly sleep or eat because of the thrill of seeing what God is doing, wondering what he will do next.

Those who study church history can point to numerous instances of revival. Just to give a few examples, revival came to England during the days of George Whitefield and the Wesley brothers and to America in the time of Jonathan Edwards and later with the preaching of Charles Finney. More recently revival occurred in Wales in the early part of the twentieth century[1] and swept the Hebrides islands of Scotland during the 1950s.[2] Revival flamed again in the Jesus People Movement in Southern California in the late 1960s and 1970s. And at the Brownsville Assembly of God

Church in Pensacola, Florida, a revival lasted more than five years, touching hundreds of thousands of lives.[3]

As much as we need these times of revival, if we're to see lasting change, revival must lead to the next step: transformation. This happens as we immerse ourselves in our Bibles, asking God's help as we search for principles to order our lives—the process Paul called having our minds renewed.[4]

This is what happened across Britain more than two centuries ago. During the time of John Wesley, revival led to transformation. You could even call it a revolution.

Wesley and the *Real* Workers' Revolution

People of all eras think they're living in the most evil times of all—that's human nature. But in many ways, John Wesley and his followers faced harsher challenges than we do today.[5] It's hard for us to realize how godless and cruel England was in the middle of the eighteenth century. Thousands poured into the cities during the Industrial Revolution, looking for a better life. Instead, they ended up as human grist for the mills. It was a time of great darkness.

Turning a Deaf Ear

No one was an advocate for the men, women, and children who worked long, dangerous hours in inhumane conditions in factories and mines, earning pitiful wages. Hunger was constant. Thousands fell prey to alcoholism, seeking escape from the daily horrors. The weak and the young became victims of tuberculosis, diphtheria, cholera, and a host of other diseases bred in overcrowded slums and overflowing privies.

Children of the poor didn't go to school. As early as age four or five they went to work in factories or mines, often working more than twelve hours a day. In textile factories children served as piecers and scavengers, tying broken threads on the moving machines and crawling under moving parts to pick up loose cotton. Some were scalped when their hair was caught; some had their hands crushed; others fell into the machinery and died. In match factories little ones died from breathing phosphorus; if they lived, the phosphorus rotted out their teeth.

Down in the mines, children pulled coal cars or hauled large baskets of coal on their backs. Mine owners could have used horses or mules, but animals cost too much to replace in the frequent cave-ins. So they used small children, who crept through spaces too narrow for adults.

Despite this cruel treatment, the church turned a deaf ear to the poor. Established churches became comfortable resting places for the affluent. Deism dominated their theology, portraying a "clockmaker" Creator uninvolved in daily human affairs. This belief, coupled with a fatalistic form of Calvinism, gave little incentive for anyone to challenge the status quo.[6]

A Heart Strangely Warmed

Thankfully, God prepared a nation changer. John Wesley was an ordained minister in the Anglican church, but things were not going well for him. He had always sought to do the right thing. While they were students at Oxford, John and his brother Charles were part of a group who called themselves "The Holy Club." Their disciplined prayer and Bible reading attracted the scorn of their fellow students, who called them "Methodists."

Despite all his efforts, though, Wesley was filled with doubt, unsure of his own salvation. He failed as a missionary when he went to the American colony of Georgia. Coming back home defeated, he was about to quit the ministry. Then something happened that changed him to his core.

On May 24, 1738, he was sitting in a Bible study in the Aldersgate district of London, listening to a Moravian preaching from Luther's preface to the book of Romans. Wesley later recorded his life-altering experience in his journal:

> About a quarter before nine, while [the speaker] was describing the change which God works in the heart through faith in Christ, I felt my heart strangely warmed. I felt I did trust in Christ, Christ alone, for salvation; and an assurance was given me that He had taken away my sins, even mine, and saved me from the law of sin and death.[7]

This changed everything. God's love filled Wesley, and he knew that his sins were really forgiven. He immediately set out to spread the good news to others.

John and his song-writing brother, Charles, believed they could reform the Church of England. However, the staunchly conservative churches gave no welcome to their emotional preaching and singing. The brothers were literally locked out of church after church. So the Wesleys took their message outside—into the open air. A shocking thing at the time, this method was being used by a friend from their Holy Club days in Oxford, George Whitefield. As the Wesleys and Whitefield preached to the poor, they lit a fire to what became one of the largest, most radical social movements of all time.

Building Blocks of Reform

While a few of John's converts came from the upper classes, the desperate were the ones who really flocked to hear him. Thousands and thousands of dirty, poor, illiterate workers heard the gospel and found hope.

The Wesley brothers soon had their hands full, trying to disciple the new converts. No church welcomed these unkempt new believers, so John started small weekly groups to teach them everyday biblical living. He traveled continually by horseback—covering 250,000 miles in his lifetime—preaching to unbelievers, organizing converts into small discipleship groups, and training lay leaders. In all he trained ten thousand small-group leaders.[8] Called "classes," those small groups became the building blocks of reform. In them, new believers were discipled and refined, learning accountability, honesty, godly living, leadership, and the value of working together for common causes.

Preventing a Bloodbath

By 1798, the Methodists, as they were called, numbered 100,000.[9] They believed that God had called them, as John Wesley said, "to reform the nation, particularly the Church, and to spread scriptural holiness over the whole land."[10] Wesley's message emphasized the "wholeness" of the gospel. It wasn't enough to save people's souls; their minds and bodies and surroundings needed transformation, too.[11]

Because of this conviction, John Wesley's ministry in Great Britain went far beyond evangelism. John opened a medical dispensary, a bookstore, a free school, and a shelter for widows. He attacked slavery before the best-known antislavery campaigner, William Wilberforce, was born. Wesley took up the causes of civil and religious freedom and awakened the conscience of the nation to the evils of exploiting the poor. He set up spinning and knitting shops and studied medicine himself so that he could help the destitute.[12]

Wesley's ministry also led to the establishment of workers' rights and safety in the workplace. Former British prime minister David Lloyd George said that for more than a hundred years Methodists were the primary leaders of the trade-union movement.[13]

One example of the godly reformers was a Bible-believing businessman, Samuel Plimsoll. He thought it was wrong that merchants overloaded their vessels, then shrugged it off when their ships sank and everyone drowned, caring only that they could make large insurance claims and recover their losses. To combat this evil, Plimsoll invented a symbol that marked a line on the ship to indicate a safe loading level. This one device, still called the Plimsoll mark, has saved thousands of lives over the years.[14]

Another evangelical, Robert Raikes, came up with the idea of Sunday schools to give working children a chance to be educated.[15] Others touched by the Wesley revival worked for reform in orphanages, mental asylums, hospitals, and prisons. Florence Nightingale and Elizabeth Fry were two of these reformers, known for developing the nursing profession and reforming prisons.[16]

John Wesley's legacy also includes the emancipation of women. Wesley treated women as spiritual equals in the Methodist movement. People of faith such as Josephine Butler, Susan B. Anthony, and Charles Finney followed in Wesley's footsteps, calling for women to have the right to higher education and vocational goals, including the ministry.[17] Former Methodists William and Catherine Booth were others who picked up Wesley's legacy, releasing thousands of women into ministry through the Salvation Army and awakening the church again to the poor outside its doors.

As these kinds of reforms took place in England, many of that nation's elite watched the French Revolution of 1789–99 in fear as it turned into a bloodbath, killing nobles, priests, and others. Maybe something similar would happen in England! It might have, but according to historian J. Wesley Bready, the renewal movement led by the Wesleys prevented it.[18] The revival that turned into transformation initiated significant political, economic, and social changes, alleviating injustice and poverty and lifting thousands of people into a more robust middle class.

Optimism and a Sense of Calling

The Wesley renewal movement didn't just affect Britain. It spread to other European nations and to America. John Wesley's followers went as missionaries to the newly emerging nation, the United States. As fast as American frontier settlements developed across the continent, Methodist circuit-riding preachers arrived on horseback. They came with a Bible in hand and other books in their bags, ready to preach and establish churches. Soon nearly every crossroads community had a Methodist group at work. The Methodists' message of free will and God's grace shaped the United States, producing optimism and a sense of divine calling.

Wesley didn't live to see all the reforms touched off by his efforts to disciple his nation. But it's hard to imagine our world today had it not been for thousands and thousands of people in small groups studying the Bible and applying it in their lives. It all began when one man had his heart strangely warmed and obeyed God and his Word, teaching his nation how to live God's way. God wants to do it again.

Chapter 5

Dare to Imagine

What if the tide were turned in your nation? What would your country look like if more and more people applied the truths of Scripture in their lives?

It might be hard to imagine a country where the majority respects God's wise intentions for his creation. I find it a little easier to picture than young people do.

I grew up in Los Angeles in a racially mixed neighborhood. It was safe to leave our doors unlocked at night. As a young boy, I rode my bicycle all over the city, and my parents didn't worry. I didn't hear about drugs like marijuana, heroin, or crack in high school; only a few kids smoked cigarettes or drank alcohol. People believed that sex was supposed to be between a man and a woman who were married to each other. If an unmarried couple got pregnant, they either got married or gave the baby up for adoption. Sexual perversions weren't spoken of; many Americans had never heard of them. Almost every marriage was "until death do us part." It was rare to know a young person who didn't have both parents at home.

Try to picture the good of that earlier era again, only much better, without its pitfalls and blind spots. What would it look like if more and more of our neighbors lived their lives according to God's ways, as revealed in the Bible? Remember, we are not looking back to any supposedly golden age but ahead to what God can accomplish in our lifetime. So dare to imagine:

- A majority would honor God and respect each other, viewing life as God's gift.
- Every mother would treasure her unborn child, and every father would provide the loving stability his child needs.
- Racism would be rare. Reconciliation and unity would bring all races and ethnic groups together.
- We wouldn't have to fear violence or theft.
- Gangs would disappear from lack of membership. Instead young people would find true community and purpose in the body of Christ.
- People would keep the streets clean. No one would scrawl graffiti on walls, freeway overpasses, or buildings.
- Most people would protect the environment, practicing good stewardship over God's creation.
- Child abuse and spousal abuse would all but disappear.
- Divorce would be extremely rare.
- Broken relationships would be restored as people repented and forgave one another.
- Corporate scandals would be all but gone.
- Businesses would seek to outdo one another with compassion initiatives.
- Politicians, officials, and judges would be true public servants.
- Billions of dollars would be freed up for public works because there would be so little corruption, fraud, or income tax evasion.
- Worker productivity would soar as addiction to alcohol, other drugs, and pornography declined and as people worked with vision, purpose, and skill.
- Empty prisons would have to be redesigned for other uses or demolished.
- We would look outward, helping people far away, sharing the gospel and giving for their physical needs.

- People would speak the truth in love. Profanity and slander would become the exception, not the norm.
- Road rage would be a peculiar phenomenon for history scholars to ponder.

What else might happen? What would your nation look like? Dare to dream, and then step out in faith to see these things become reality.

It Could Be Your Nation

When we see a nation marked by characteristics like these and blessed with good fortune and freedom, we will invariably discover in the nation's history people like John Wesley who sought God and spent time in his Book, looking for ways to disciple their countries.

Today God is looking for others who will take his Word seriously, searching it as a textbook to transform nations and affect their generation. This could be you. Spending time in his presence, on your knees with his Word, will change every area of your life. As you do this, you will influence those around you. And as more and more people do this, a whole nation will be changed. It could be your nation.

Lip service to God doesn't change lives or nations. Owning a Bible that we never read won't change us either. It takes reading the Bible and obeying God by the power of his Holy Spirit. As we obey him and his Word, we grow in character. God's Word becomes part of us, the standard for all of our lives. This is what changes a nation.

Who Are the Nation Builders?

Lately many leaders and pundits have been discussing whose role it is to build nations. Their discussions fill the airwaves, Internet, and print outlets, but I haven't heard a clear answer from any of them. Who, then, are the nation builders? Armies? Peacekeepers? Government leaders? The United Nations? NGOs? To answer this question, we need to define our terms. What is a nation, anyway?

When we say "nation," we often mean the *state*—the political organization or the government. We think in terms of boundaries and passports and flags. But the Bible gives us a different understanding of nations. We see in Genesis how families became tribes, which then became nations, which became separated by language differences and spread out over all the earth. Looking at it this way, nations are simply families or tribes of people. They share a common heritage and language and beliefs and ways of doing things that we call "culture."

The word *nation* in the New Testament is the Greek word *ethné*, which is closer to our term, *ethnic group*. I believe this is still the primary way God looks at nations—ethnic groups made up of families and tribes—people who have a common culture and language. Nations are *peoples*.

If we want to build nations, then, we must build up people—families, tribes, ethnic groups, entire countries. That's the job Jesus gives us in Matthew 28:19. He says his followers are to be nation builders. But how are we to do this?

Seven Places to Start

Where do we start? That's the question I was asking God in 1975. I was concerned over the direction my country and other countries were heading. How could we turn our nations around? How could we see basic foundations of morality and goodness restored?

That summer I was in Colorado, vacationing with my family in the San Juan Mountains. We were enjoying a cabin that a friend made available. Early one morning as I sat beside the unlit fireplace, the Lord quietly spoke to me. *There are seven areas of society that are like classrooms to disciple nations.* I grabbed paper and pen as the thoughts came to me quickly, fully formed. I could hardly write the seven areas fast enough on my yellow pad:

- Family
- Religion (church and mission)
- Education
- Celebration (arts, entertainment, sports)
- Public communication (media)
- Economy (including business, science, and technology)
- Government

That's interesting, I thought as I carefully folded the paper and put it in my pocket. Later that day, the forest ranger came to our cabin on his motorbike, stirring a small cloud of dust. "Mr. Cunningham," he said, "there's a phone call for you back at the ranger station."

The call was from a friend who said Bill and Vonette Bright, the founders of Campus Crusade for Christ, were in Boulder and wanted to meet with my wife, Darlene, and me.

The next day, a friend flew our family over the Rockies in his Cessna Centurion. We sat down to visit with Dr. and Mrs. Bright. I was just about to take the yellow paper out of my pocket to share with Bill when he said, "Loren, the Lord has shown me several ways we can change our nation."

He unfolded a piece of paper and read from it. His list was virtually the same as mine! Then I showed him my list.

I knew this wasn't just a word for me or for YWAM. It was for the body of Christ. A few days later, I spoke at a cathedral filled with hundreds of young people in Hamburg, Germany, giving them the seven spheres God wanted us to target to turn our nations around.

A few weeks later, Darlene heard Dr. Francis Schaeffer, founder of L'Abri Fellowship, in a TV interview. Dr. Schaeffer gave the same list of areas for believers to target.

Wouldn't you agree that whenever God speaks to three people in three different parts of the body of Christ with the same message, he is trying to get his message through to his people? What I didn't know then was how key men and women of God have been targeting these same spheres for hundreds of years, to see their nations transformed. In the next few chapters we're going to look at just a few of these people. Their stories are powerful. They are heroes. They are real nation builders.

Part 2

Portraits of
Transformation

Chapter 6

A True Nation Builder: William Carey

India

It's hard to imagine what William Carey saw as he stepped off the boat in India in 1793. Carey, a shoemaker, pastor, and self-taught linguist, found much that desperately needed to be reformed in every area of Indian society. Ruth and Vishal Mangal-wadi give us a picture of what India was like at that time in their book *The Legacy of William Carey: A Model for the Transformation of a Culture*, from which the following descriptions have been gleaned.[1]

When Carey arrived, India was held in the grip of the worst deception. Hinduism guaranteed that only a few people, those at the very top of society, enjoyed material possessions and education. The caste system held the rest in perpetual slavery. Indians considered this the rightful order of things. Lower classes were atoning for sins they had committed in previous lives.

Hindu teachers said there was no difference between them and god. Man only imagined he was separate from the deity. Therefore, anything they did was divine. This belief divorced religion from

51

morality, making it possible for Indians to be extremely religious while at the same time doing terrible things.

When Carey came to India, nearly three thousand years of Hinduism had brought the civilization to near collapse. Learning had almost ceased; ordinary education scarcely existed. The "all pervasive culture of bribery" had pushed lending rates from 36 percent to as much as 100 percent, making investment impossible.

Human rights were nonexistent. Women were held in contempt. For example, Hinduism sanctioned female infanticide, child marriage, polygamy, widow burning (*suttee*), and euthanasia. A woman's only hope was to serve her man well and possibly merit being reborn as a man. Lepers were buried alive or burned to death to ensure a better rebirth in the next life. Sick babies were hung in a basket for three days without any care to see if they would overcome the "evil spirit." Every winter, parents pushed their children down mud banks where the Hooghly River meets the sea, to either drown or be eaten by crocodiles. People considered mothers to be highly devout for sacrificing their children to Mother Ganges in this way.

We could understand if William Carey had looked around him and decided just to concentrate on the spiritual rescue of those individuals he could reach. But he didn't stop with evangelizing (the Mark 16:15 half of the Great Commission). He also threw himself into the other half (Matthew 28:19). Carey began the monumental task of discipling India. We don't have space to explore all that this remarkable nation builder did. For that, I'd recommend you read any of the Mangalwadis' excellent books. But let's quickly see how William Carey made an impact on each of the seven spheres in India.

Family

William Carey tackled the job of reforming India's families. He realized that no country could be free if its women were oppressed. First he lobbied to see the killing of unwanted babies outlawed, achieving that victory in 1804. It was harder to root out the horrific practice of burning widows alive on their husbands' funeral pyres. But Carey finally saw that outlawed in 1829.

Religion

Of course, Carey and his close circle of coworkers did much in the area of religion, building the church of Jesus Christ on Indian soil. They started the Baptist churches of India, which continue to multiply today. Carey also founded Serampore College, which trained the first Indian pastors. And he oversaw the translation of the Bible into nearly forty languages so that Indians could read it in their mother tongues.

Education

Carey started dozens of schools for children of all castes and for women. As already mentioned, he launched Serampore College, which was Asia's first liberal arts college with teaching in vernacular languages. He authored the first Sanskrit dictionary for scholars and started the first lending libraries in India.

Celebration (the Arts)

The tireless missionary even had a hand in developing the arts in India. Carey promoted literature by translating and publishing great Indian classics. He elevated the Bengali language, previously considered "fit only for demons and women," into the foremost literary language of India. He wrote Bengali gospel ballads, capitalizing on the Indians' love for musical recitations, to effectively communicate Christ's message.

Public Communication

Carey also brought mass media to India, setting up the first printing press and teaching Indians how to use it, as well as how to make their own paper. He established the first newspaper ever printed in an Asian language. He believed that "above all forms of truth and faith, Christianity seeks free discussion." His English newspaper published articles that helped bring about many of India's social reforms in the first half of the nineteenth century.

Economy

It's hard to imagine where India's economy would be today if Carey hadn't introduced the idea of savings banks and pushed for reasonable interest rates and foreign investment. But that wasn't all he did to benefit the nation's economy. In technology, he introduced the steam engine to India. In medicine, he led the campaign for humane treatment of lepers, demonstrating a biblical concern for individuals. In science, he founded the Agri-Horticultural Society, did a systematic survey of agriculture, and brought in the teaching of modern astronomy to offset Indians' bondage to astrology. A dedicated botanist, Carey also published India's first books on science and natural history. He wasn't like the Hindus, who taught that physical reality was to be denied as illusion. Instead, he believed the Bible, where God looked at creation and said it was good.[2] Carey remembered, "All thy works shall praise thee, O LORD."[3] Because the Word of God teaches that man is to have authority over nature,[4] he wrote essays supporting forestry conservation fifty years before the government did so.[5]

Government

Some of Carey's most spectacular success came in the sphere of government, where he faced formidable obstacles. We need to understand that when Carey first came to India, he was doing something illegal. The British East India Company, in league with the Crown, had banned all missionary activity. Some might look at reforms that eventually came to India and think the British colonial government was responsible. They would be wrong. The British had been in India since 1600 but had done nothing to bring reform.[6]

The British believed in leaving existing religious forces in place on the grounds that it would be easier to control the colony. Before Carey and his Bible-believing friends came onto the scene, all the colonial government did was exploit India; it did not think of benefiting the Indian people.[7]

It was the followers of Jesus who kept hammering away on these issues. Believers back home in Britain, such as William Wilberforce in Parliament, joined Carey in pleading the case for India. Finally, they persuaded the English conscience to adopt a more "civil service" in their colony, to initiate reforms.[8]

One big battle Carey fought all his life still hasn't been won. The caste system remains in place, keeping hundreds of millions in abject poverty with no way out.

Recently world leaders have been pleased to see economic growth in India—boomlets in the private sector with new buildings and businesses springing up, even a modest growth of the middle class. But these leaders seem blind to the fact that more than 160 million Indians are shut off from any possibility of participating in this new economy. The Dalits, formerly known as "untouchables," make up 17 percent of India's population.[9] The term *untouchable* is quite literal; if a Dalit touches someone or something belonging to a person of a higher caste, that person must go through a ritual cleansing. Under the caste system, Dalits have no hope of a better future. The caste system bars them from any occupation but the most demeaning, such as cleaning out public latrines, and Hindu custom forbids Dalit children to go to school. Dalits spend their short miserable lives trying not to starve, raising their families in horrific slums, or even living right on the sidewalks of India's cities.[10] Others taking part in India's new economic growth merely step over or around their bodies, hurrying to their jobs. The fight against the caste system must continue.

However, I am still encouraged to see real changes on the horizon. The church in India is one of the fastest growing in the world. Thousands are deciding to believe in Jesus every day. According to a student of Indian church growth, the Rev. Dr. J. N. Manokaran, an estimated sixty million Indians believe in Christ, worshiping in 400,000 churches and house churches. Three hundred thousand pastors, missionaries, and evangelists are bringing in a vast harvest of believers and working to disciple their nation. Joshua Pillai of Dawn Ministries reports that Indian pastors are planting more than fifty thousand churches every year. That's forty-one new churches a day![11] Indian believers are also reaching far beyond their borders. Tens of thousands of Indian missionaries are going to other lands, as well as working cross-culturally within their own nation.[12] Some experts believe that when in-country missionaries are counted, India ranks second in the world for sending the most missionaries.[13]

Carey laid a strong foundation. Yet across this vast nation, hundreds of millions are not transformed in their thinking. They still cling to the old ways. India needs more nation builders to carry on what William Carey set in motion.

Chapter 7

A Man You Need to Meet: Abraham Kuyper

The Netherlands

Many have heard of William Carey. But not many know about Abraham Kuyper (pronounced Ky-per), another nation builder. Allow me to introduce you to this Dutchman, a preacher who became prime minister of the Netherlands. He has a lot to teach us—particularly, how to bear faithful witness to Jesus Christ in a pluralistic society. Let's go back to Europe in the middle of the nineteenth century and meet this amazing man.[1]

In Kuyper's day, the continent was still recovering from major upheavals, such as the blood-soaked French Revolution and the Napoleonic wars. Two major ideas emerged in this turbulent time: Marxism and the theological liberalism of the Romantic era. Most of the bigger European universities devoted themselves to rationalism and humanism, the beliefs that man could find truth within himself and solve his problems without God. These dominating thoughts also ruled the seminaries that trained young ministers. So when Abraham Kuyper decided to become a minister, he went to a Dutch university where his professors taught him that Jesus was just a man and the Bible a collection of myths.

Envying His Parishioners' Faith

By the time he completed his theological training and took his first pastorate, Kuyper had little or no belief in a personal, active God. But as the months went by, he was surprised to find himself envying the faith of the common people in his little country church. Soon one of his own parishioners led him to Christ as his personal Savior.

Using his persuasive intellectual gifts and an almost super-human energy, Kuyper immediately devoted himself to bringing the Dutch church back to its biblical foundations. He accepted the pastorate of a large church in Utrecht in 1867. While serving as a full-time minister, he also became a journalist, writing political and religious columns for the newspaper. He ended up serving as chief editor for two separate papers—a weekly and a daily—for forty years. But that wasn't all. He also worked as an educator and class-room teacher, a political activist, a member of Parliament, and finally, prime minister of the Netherlands, continuing in all of these vocations, except that of prime minister, for decades.

Finding the Spheres

It's little wonder that Kuyper's physical strength gave out. In 1875, just one year after he was elected to Parliament, he had to take two years off to recover his health, which he did on a furlough in Switzerland. While Kuyper was there, praying and searching the Scriptures, God began to give him a most important understanding. Exactly one hundred years before the Lord spoke to me and to Dr. Bill Bright about the spheres of society, he showed Abraham Kuyper the same thing. I don't know whether Dr. Bright had heard of Abraham Kuyper in 1975. I had not.

Kuyper called it "sphere sovereignty." This concept would show Christ's followers how to bring the lordship of Jesus into every area of the modern nations of Europe.

When Kuyper studied the writings of John Calvin, he learned that God wasn't to be neatly categorized in the "religious" box, open only on Sunday. God was to be the Lord over all areas of life, just as the church prayed every week: *Thy kingdom come, thy will be done on earth as it is in heaven.* Jeremiah 27:5 says God made the world and everything in it, and he gives it to the one who pleases him. *All* spheres are owned by God, and *all* of society needs the teachings of Christ, to counter the sin-bent tendencies of humans, to produce love and wholeness.

Not a Theocracy

Kuyper also agreed with Calvin that the church as an institution should not *rule* over the other spheres directly, even though the whole of society was accountable to God. No, Kuyper thought, we aren't to establish a theocracy. God respects our free will. He also respects the separation of powers. Faith could not be enforced.

But neither should the state dominate, as the humanistic socialists proposed. Nor were individuals to simply do their own thing, as more extreme proponents of democratic liberalism and anarchists were saying. Instead, Kuyper understood that God designed people to operate within "spheres," with limited authority for each one. (This understanding is similar to the division of powers between prophets, priests, and kings in ancient Israel, or between governmental executive, legislative, and judicial powers in modern countries.)

Kuyper saw five distinct spheres: self-government (the individual, accountable to God), family government (parents were given primary responsibility for the education and training of their children), church government (managing church affairs and leadership, along with church discipline), civil government (given the divine mandate to "bear the sword" in order to limit the effect of man's fallen condition), and societal government (voluntary associations, such as clubs, businesses, societies, and organizations).[2]

Jesus, Lord of All

While Kuyper emphasized that each sphere should be founded on principles from God's Word, he taught that Jesus himself should be Lord in all the spheres, with each sphere directly responsible to God. No sphere should overstep its God-given authority in relating to other spheres. Rather, individuals should bring God's influence and teaching into whatever area of life they were working in.

You can see the wisdom God gave Kuyper in setting these out as interrelated yet limited spheres of authority. For whenever the institutional church intrudes into matters of state, you have religious tyranny. If the state intrudes into family spheres or dictates religious affairs, you have political tyranny. If the church intrudes into family spheres, you end up with a religious cult. Instead, we should have division of powers between these God-given spheres of authority, with individual freedom within an orderly society.

Foundations for Modern Holland

Returning from his health furlough where God revealed these insights, Kuyper threw himself into even greater activity back in the Netherlands. He put great effort into bringing the influence of the gospel into the media, politics, the school, the church, and the family. He went back to work on both newspapers, using them to teach his readers to apply truths from the Bible in every area of life. He reorganized a political party, energizing a growing number of lower middle-class people to bring reforms based on biblical teaching.

In education, Kuyper and his colleagues fought for the right to have "free schools." They believed parents should have the right to send their children to publicly funded schools that taught according to their particular worldview—including "Schools with the Bible." In fact, this pattern continues today in the Netherlands, not only in their educational system but also in newspapers, trade unions, political parties, and broadcasting companies that reflect a spectrum of worldviews.

In 1880, Kuyper opened a university in Amsterdam—the *Vereniging voor Christelijk Wetenschappelijk Onderwijs*, or Association for Christian Scientific Education. He became its first rector, founding it on the lordship of Jesus Christ. The faculty encouraged students to love the Lord with their minds and carry his truth into every sphere of the nation. Kuyper started with four professors and only five students. Today that school calls itself the *Vrije Universiteit*, or Free University. It's one of the largest universities in the world. Over the years it has produced, or had on its faculty, some of the leading figures of the nation. While many things have changed, the university still recognizes that its origins are rooted in the Christian faith. It emphasizes its Christian standards and values, especially through social involvement.[3]

Working for the Future

Kuyper returned to Parliament in 1894 with renewed vigor, launching a period of political activity that amazed friends and foes. The queen of Holland asked Kuyper to become prime minister in 1901. In his opening speech, Kuyper declared his intention to build the nation on biblical principles. He introduced many social reforms in his political career, securing the rights of the poor, minorities, and workers. His influence spread internationally, as he was called to mediate peace between the British and the Boers at war in South Africa.

Like Wesley in England and Carey in India, Abraham Kuyper worked for the future. As energetic and intelligent as he was, he knew he couldn't reform an entire nation alone. He wrote in one of his newspaper columns:

> We are working for the long haul. We aim not for the apparent triumph of the moment, but for the ultimate success of our cause. The question is not what influence we have now, but what power we will exercise in half a century; not how few we have now, but how many of the young generation will take a stand for our cause.[4]

Short-term Thinking, Long-term Failure

Of course, not everyone cares about generations to come. We read in the Bible about King Hezekiah. He was a good king, one of the best. But he committed a serious sin against God. The prophet came to him and in effect said, "Your generation will be safe, but your son's generation will reap what you and the people have done in sin."[5]

Hezekiah rejoiced when the prophet said that. Why? Because he would be spared God's judgment. He should have wept for the pain of future generations.

In our time, too many of us are like Hezekiah, living with a short-range view. We only want to think about what we can get for ourselves right now. Instead, we should be like Wesley, Carey, and Kuyper, thinking in terms of three or four generations hence. We should be living our lives in a way that our children's children will be blessed.

Please don't misunderstand what I'm about to say. But a major factor in our short-term mentality is an over-the-top emphasis of end-time prophecy.

A few years ago while on a flight, I was talking with a fellow passenger who was one of the world's leading environmentalists. I asked her how we were doing overall in overcoming pollution. She said, "We're making headway motivating every major group but one—evangelical Christians." She went on to explain that this is because evangelicals believe Jesus is returning any minute and that this has kept them from caring about pollution. "If we could just get this group on board," she said, "we could turn the situation around."

I knew what she meant. I've heard it described as "end-times paralysis." Many in the church are focused only on the present. They believe if they plan for the future, that means they aren't having faith that Jesus is coming soon.

Some of us had believing grandparents and great-grandparents like this. They were convinced there would be no future generations. They focused all their attention on simply getting people converted before the Second Coming. They withdrew from politics, the arts, education, and other influential areas and from the effort it took to maintain a godly presence in those critical arenas. Instead of training their children for leadership in the world, they preached against such participation.

"We'd Rather Send Our Young People to Hell"

I recently heard a dramatic example of the church's withdrawal. Dr. William Dyrness, professor of theology and culture at Fuller Seminary, tells of a producer at Twentieth Century Fox in the 1930s. The producer wrote letters to several evangelical colleges, asking them to send their graduates to become screenwriters, to help make good, wholesome movies. Did the church capture this golden opportunity? No. One college president wrote back saying he'd sooner send their young people to hell itself than send them to Hollywood.[6]

We must recapture leadership in influential areas of society, as Abraham Kuyper did in the Netherlands and William Carey did in India. We must not let our beliefs about prophecy and the end times keep us from doing everything we can to disciple nations, including our own. Jesus told us to occupy until he comes.[7] That's active, not passive. When Jesus returns, he should find us busy bringing every part of the earth into his kingdom.

Chapter 8

Skiing with Bibles:
Hans Nielsen Hauge

Norway

One of the greatest nation builders grew up on a farm in Norway. Many think this country got rich simply because of its extensive oil wealth in the North Sea. But there's a lot more to the story. I've observed great poverty in other oil-producing nations. Corrupt despots often rule such countries, with their citizens languishing without freedom. Norway is different. Its blessings go wide and deep because of the character of its people. And that character is largely the result of one Norwegian who taught the people the Word of God in the nineteenth century.

A few years ago, I had the privilege of meeting with King Harald V of Norway. It was 1995. I received the invitation through the Royal Appointments Secretary, who had heard me speak when he was a teenager. He had read all of my books and passed them on to the king. Alv Magnus, the leader of YWAM in Norway, went with me to meet the king at the Royal Palace.

Before we were ushered in, I asked the appointments secretary how much time we would be given with His Majesty. "Oh, he will let you know when to leave," he replied quickly.

A heavy door swung open to an expansive meeting room paneled in rich wood, hung with paintings in gilded frames. Windows looked out over broad, sloping grounds, with the city of Oslo in the distance beyond the gates. The king stood and greeted us warmly, then seated us on either side of him. I had thought earlier what to say to the king, to make the most of this moment.

After preliminary introductions, I said, "Your Majesty, when your grandfather was a child, Norway was the poorest nation in Europe." The king agreed. Not only was Norway poor then, but its people were mostly uneducated and had very little freedom.

"But now, Your Majesty, it's just been announced that Norway is the richest nation per capita on earth. You have a wonderful educational system with 100 percent literacy, and your people enjoy great freedom. How do you explain such rapid change in such a short time?"

King Harald reached over and touched my arm. "Mr. Cunningham, I don't know! I'm asked that question by ambassadors all the time and I just say, 'I don't know.'"

"Would you like to hear about the person who changed your country, Your Majesty?" I asked.

The story goes back more than two hundred years, to a young man named Hans Nielsen Hauge (pronounced *How-gah*). Most people outside Norway have never heard of him. And inside Norway, many people are like their king—only aware of Hauge as a sort of folk hero of the past. But the impact of his life was enormous. Alv Magnus, my fellow guest that day in the palace, had written his master's thesis about Hauge. So Alv and I told the king how one young man made a great difference in his country.[1]

We stayed a long time, as King Harald seemed fascinated with the story. When we finally received the signal that our time was over, we walked out to find the waiting room had stacked up with ambassadors and officials waiting their turn with the king.

Here's the story King Harald found so interesting that he kept all the ambassadors waiting.

Barely Able to Feed Themselves

Hauge lived from 1771 to 1824. He was a farmer's son, raised in a family that honored the Bible. He was sensitive to spiritual matters but never felt good enough to be saved. Hans was clever with his hands, and even as a young man he began to prosper from his work. However, he felt uneasy because he recognized that he was being motivated more by the pursuit of worldly goods than his love of God.

One day, when Hauge was twenty-five years old, his life was turned upside down. On April 5, 1796, he was singing a hymn as he worked in the field. Suddenly, he felt his heart lifted to God, and his mind flooded with new understanding. In an instant he knew that God had accepted him. His sins were forgiven. He also knew that he must preach God's Word throughout Norway.

When Hauge began his ministry, Norway was barely able to feed itself. Though there were a few rich merchants and landowners, most Norwegians were peasants. Jeff Fountain, YWAM's European director, tells how famine broke out at times, forcing the people to make bread from the bark of trees. It wasn't uncommon to find the bodies of those who had starved to death beside the road. The situation wasn't likely to change either, since they had few schools and no universities. After hundreds of years of subjugation by her neighbors, the country was little more than fishing villages and a patchwork of subsistence farms. People didn't have personal freedom in the Danish-Norwegian kingdom either. They weren't allowed to meet in public or travel about the country without the government's permission.

A Threat to the Establishment

Hauge, however, ignored these restrictions. He began to go everywhere, on foot and on skis, sharing his newfound faith with great power. As he crisscrossed the country, his radical preaching shocked the churches of his time. Many had fallen prey to rationalism or to lethargy. Yet God reached out through this farmer-preacher and warmed the hearts of countless Norwegians, winning them to himself.

The authorities jailed Hauge for conducting religious meetings without the supervision of parish pastors. Hauge answered his critics, saying that the Bible admonished believers to build each other up. Indeed, when Hauge preached, many listened and believed. Between 1796 and 1804, Hauge distributed the Bible from village to village, seeding the entire country with God's Book.

Excitement and new hope broke out in impoverished Norway. In less than three decades, Hauge launched more than one thousand home groups within the state church, in a nation of only 800,000.[2] As believers met in home groups to pray and study, they grew closer to God and one another. They held one another accountable to a new standard based on The Book. As Joseph Shaw says in his biography of Hauge, *Pulpit under the Sky*, "God made new people out of them and new places out of the communities where they lived."[3]

Hauge's ministry and the growing revival alarmed officials, clergy, and the upper classes. They found Hauge's message unsavory. Not only that—the very fact that a farmer was preaching at all was revolutionary and unacceptable! Even worse, this man was inspiring and training other peasants to leave their "proper place" and do the same.

So Hauge and other lay preachers he recruited were imprisoned, again and again. Hauge was arrested eleven times in seven years.

Creating Wealth through Righteous Commerce

Whether in or out of prison, Hauge continued to serve God and disciple his nation. To reach more people, he wrote books. Besides writing books of religious instruction, he wrote about how to educate children, how to create wealth through righteous commerce, and other subjects he found in God's Word.

As Hauge delved into the Bible, he was absolutely practical about life here on earth. He found The Book packed with principles for everything humanity faces. He taught that God's Word is to be our "most holy treasure above all other things in this world."[4]

He preached that all we own and all that we are come from God. The Lord expects us to be good stewards of what he has given us. Because the Creator made every person in his image, Hauge encouraged everyone to create wealth through honest work. He helped the poor find ways to support themselves. He told his followers to use their means to influence their country for God.

Hauge didn't just teach the people what the Bible says about commerce; he also put it into practice. He started many businesses. On one site alone, he built a paper mill, a stamping mill, a bone mill, a flour mill, a tannery, and a foundry. In addition, he helped direct believers to vocational opportunities in towns where they could make a difference. By doing so, this preacher-merchant improved the economy of the entire country.

Learning How to Read

Hauge saw the potential of printing to spread the gospel and teach believers. So he learned how to print and bind books. He wrote and published books of all kinds—thirty-three in his lifetime. As his writing became popular, more people became literate so they could read his books. During his first eight years of ministry, Hauge became the biggest publisher of his time. More than 200,000 copies of his books were distributed up and down the country—quite remarkable in a population of 800,000.[5]

Training Peasants for Leadership

The revival began to transform Norway. As Shaw observes, though "they themselves were not fully conscious of it...Hauge and the other simple lay preachers were hurling a challenge at a whole system."[6]

As Hauge continued to recruit fellow lay preachers from the peasant class, the movement spread swiftly. Ordinary people taught and encouraged one another, developing into communicators and leaders. Peasants whose world had been limited to one village or one valley began to relate to people across the country, creating a greater sense of national identity. Farmers migrated to towns and became craftsmen. Some of Hauge's converts pooled their money and started new businesses—textile factories, printing houses, and paper mills. As they wrote letters back and forth with others in the Hauge movement, they learned all sorts of subjects, including more progressive methods of agriculture. They even began to affect the government. When believers saw what the Bible said about government, they sought to take part. They used people skills they had learned in Hauge's small groups to get elected to Parliament.

Norwegian believers increasingly reflected Christ's character, influencing their own spheres of the culture: home, work, and social circles. They began to disciple society. And little by little Norway changed.

The Darkest Years

These changes threatened the elite. In October 1804, the authorities imprisoned Hauge again, putting him in chains for preaching without proper authority. He wouldn't be a free man for ten long years.

Hauge didn't intend to be a political threat—he was merely pursuing a nation built on biblical truth in every area. But officials thought he was a dangerous man. His teachings and the spiritual revival he stirred were changing the whole order of the country. They kept him in chains, breaking him in body. However, they couldn't stop the changes he initiated, changes that continued throughout Norway while Hauge sat in his cell.

As his imprisonment dragged on, his health failed, and at times, his spirit. He thought everyone had forgotten him. Ironically, during this term of solitary confinement, the government temporarily released Hauge because they needed his expertise to establish salt refineries on the coast. The Napoleonic Wars cut off their normal supply of salt, which their food supply depended on for preservation. So in 1809, Hauge was let out of prison long enough to solve the crisis. He investigated the best locations, searching out where the salt content of the sea water was highest. He helped establish several salt factories. Then the authorities sent him back to prison.

Finally, in December 1814 he was a free man. Though he was only forty-four years old, the long years in prison had broken his health. He spent his later years on his farm, teaching and writing.

The man who has been called "God's gift to Norway" worked to disciple his nation until the end, dying at age fifty-three. During his lifetime he had covered more than ten thousand miles by foot and by skis, circulating the Bible and his books.[7]

Taking the Long View

The wealth and freedom of Norway can clearly be traced to Hauge. A nation changed, beginning with one man. As Shaw notes, Hauge's biblical teaching and work "struck one of the earliest blows against the tyranny of an economic system which for centuries had been the monopoly of the upper classes."[8] Ultimately, some of Hauge's converts pursued Norwegian independence. They helped draft a new constitution for Norway at Eidsvoll in 1814. Hauge's followers made the country one of the most free on earth, and they did it based on biblical principles.

Hauge's heritage reached other lands as well, for Norway began to send out thousands of missionaries. It remains one of the greatest missionary-sending nations in the world.

Hauge didn't live long enough to see Norway become rich or a great missionary nation. But he was the one who started the process. If we want to change nations, we might not see the end results in our lifetime. However, the Bible promises us that if we make godly choices, the results will follow to the third and fourth generations. In some cases blessings extend to a thousand generations.[9] We shouldn't aim only to make a difference today. We should plant the seeds for a renewed world for our children, our grandchildren, and beyond, like Hauge did.

Chapter 9

An "Overnight" Success Story

South Korea

One of the greatest turnarounds in history happened in Korea during the twentieth century. But our story begins back in the fifteenth century with a Korean king named Sejong.

King Sejong said he had a word from heaven that his people were poor because they couldn't read. In those days, reading Korean required memorizing many thousands of Chinese characters. This put reading out of reach for the poor. Only the elite had the luxury of education. So King Sejong, along with a few wise men, invented a new, simplified phonetic writing system called *hangeul*. The new alphabet was originally called *hunmin jeongeum*, or "the correct sounds for the instruction of the people."[1]

The king's efforts soon attracted enemies. The court scribes saw this simplified writing system as a direct threat to their livelihood. They despised the alphabet precisely because it was so easy to learn. They mocked hangeul as suitable only for women and children. The scribes burned most of the king's papers, and the Korean people stayed illiterate and poor.

Until modern times, the vast majority of scholars and upper-class Koreans continued to use the old, more difficult Chinese script. They associated hangeul with people of low status. Yet, somehow the hangeul script survived centuries of neglect until the arrival of God's Book.

The Blood of the Martyrs

Known as the "Hermit Kingdom," Korea resisted those who came bringing God's Book. When Catholic missionaries arrived in 1784, they faced indifference, persecution, and martyrdom. But they succeeded in planting the church in Korea. In 1866, eighty-two years after the arrival of the first missionaries, Koreans massacred ten thousand Catholic believers.[2]

A year before that massacre, a Protestant missionary named Robert Thomas tried to land in Korea. He managed to throw a bundle of Bibles into the crowd before they beat him to death.[3]

God's Word in King Sejong's Script

Outside the country, a few Koreans became believers and returned with the Word. One was Suh Sang-Yoon. Scottish missionaries had led him to Christ in 1876 in Manchuria. Suh Sang-Yoon helped translate the New Testament into Korean, using hangeul, King Sejong's four-hundred-year-old simplified script. Then he brought Gospel portions back to his homeland.[4] In addition, Protestant missionaries came in the latter part of the nineteenth century, spreading God's Word and starting schools, clinics, and universities. The Word was planted and beginning to spread.

But still, Buddhism and spirit religions dominated the Hermit Kingdom. At the beginning of the twentieth century, Korean believers numbered one-half of one percent of the population—only 42,700.[5]

Keeping the Language and Faith Alive

The worst of times came with the dawning of the twentieth century. A brutal occupation by Japan for thirty-six years threatened to crush Korea's very identity. The Japanese outlawed the Korean language from the schools and any public use. It was the underground, persecuted church that kept the language alive, teaching from Bibles printed in hangeul despite persecution. The punishment for teaching the Bible in the Korean language was imprisonment. Some were even killed for teaching God's Word.

Sadly, when the Japanese were driven out at the end of World War II, an even crueler power took over in the north—a dictator named Kim Il Sung. He killed many thousands of Korean believers. In 1950, he invaded the southern part of Korea, trying to forcibly unite the peninsula under communism. His attack touched off the Korean War. While the conflict lasted only three years, it tore the country apart, saturating the Korean peninsula in blood and leaving it divided. An estimated five million people were killed or wounded or remain missing, with more than half of these casualties from the civilian population. The war ripped ten million people from their families and left one hundred thousand children orphaned.[6] The country lay stripped bare and in great poverty.

Praying for a Bicycle

When I visited South Korea for the first time in 1971, poverty and military rule still plagued the nation. I'll never forget that visit. In Seoul, I spoke at Dr. David Yonggi Cho's church. At that time the church had "only" six thousand members. I stood before these Korean believers and said what God had impressed upon me: Korea was going to become a great nation, sending missionaries all over the world. Afterward, several believers came up to me, greeting me with *"Kahm sah hahm nee tah,"* which means "thank you." Then they politely disagreed with my prediction. They were too poor to go out as missionaries. Besides, their government made it impossible for them to get passports for international travel.

Both of these misgivings were real. South Korea was indeed poor. And ten years earlier, the military had seized power. For decades the people had suffered. Since the moment of my arrival I saw the grip of poverty on the people. One of the things I noticed as my plane touched down was the absence of trees in the countryside. We learned that people were so desperate for fuel during the long years of warfare that they cut down all their trees. As I traveled around Seoul, I noticed it was filled with poorly constructed apartment buildings and garbage-filled alleyways. Overcrowded buses labored down the streets, while dozens of small, beat-up cabs darted about, along with lots of military vehicles. Very few private citizens could own an automobile. In fact, I didn't see one car parked outside Dr. Cho's church. Dr. Cho himself had prayed and trusted God for a bicycle so that he could get around to his parishioners more easily.

From Poverty to Success in Thirty Years

Thirty years later I returned to speak in Pastor Cho's church. As we drove into Seoul that evening, I looked about me, amazed at the changes. Koreans had a new problem, with thousands and thousands of Hyundais, Daewoos, and Kias jostling in bumper-to-bumper traffic on the freeway. High-rise buildings—layers of offices and luxury apartments for the newly affluent—speared the sky. I looked closer and saw something that warmed my heart—neon blue crosses on the tops of countless churches on both sides of the freeway glowed in the pale evening light.

When it was time for me to speak on Sunday morning at Dr. Cho's church, again I could scarcely believe the difference. Yoido Full Gospel Church now had more than seven hundred thousand members, making it the largest church in the world.[7] And since hundreds of thousands now owned cars, the parishioners had to park in distant parking lots and ride shuttle buses to the church sanctuary.

What I saw firsthand in Seoul is now being reported in news articles and reports. Recent economic growth has made South Korea an "Asian Tiger," with the world's sixteenth largest economy.[8] Rather than military rule, South Korea now has a civilian, democratic government. And what about that unbelievable prediction the Lord compelled me to make from Dr. Cho's pulpit in 1971—that Korea would send out many missionaries? With a population of just forty-eight million, South Korea now sends the second greatest number of missionaries overseas, only behind the United States.[9]

A Low Voice with Wisdom

According to a recent *Seoul Times* article, South Korea now has more than twelve thousand missionaries abroad.[10] This is twice the number per capita the United States sends, even though the United States is known as a majority Christian nation. The Presbyterian Onnuri Church commits itself to missions the way many churches do in Korea. The church was founded nineteen years ago mainly to train missionaries. Now five hundred from this one church are serving in fifty-three countries. Korean missionaries work in many nations, with a significant number in Middle Eastern countries, where it's often difficult to evangelize. One such missionary speaks of working in a "low voice and with wisdom," in order to reach people in such situations.[11] The South Korean church is also reaching into China, and even into North Korea.

Talking Back to the TV

What happened? How could one country's fortunes change in less than thirty years? South Korea's economic growth came hand in hand with a rapid growth of the church—one of the greatest in the history of the world.

I was in Mumbai (Bombay) recently in a hotel room, listening to the Indian finance minister speaking on TV. He said, "If South Korea can become a wealthy nation in only twenty-five years, so can India." I blurted out loud to the TV set, "Not without Jesus!" For that's why South Korea is succeeding.[12]

One-third or more South Koreans now follow Christ.[13] That means Korean believers grew from one-half of one percent to at least one-third of the country in less than one hundred years! I can't think of a more dramatic growth of the church anytime in history.

Massive Prayer Meetings at Dawn

The soil for Korea's dramatic church growth was watered by the blood of martyrs, many thousands in the nineteenth and twentieth centuries. A story I'll never forget told of soldiers herding Korean believers—men, women, and children—into a church. The soldiers barred the doors and set the building on fire. The believers sang as they died, their hymns rising above the sounds of crackling fire and collapsing beams.

Korean followers of Jesus who survived persecution seemed girded with steel. Rising from these roots, Koreans gave themselves to prayer and Bible study in an unusual way. If you visit South Korea today, you'll find hundreds of thousands filling churches every morning at 5:00 AM to pray and read their Bibles for two hours before heading to work. Weekly all-night prayer meetings and spiritual retreats to fast and pray are common. I have visited the Osanri Prayer Mountain outside Seoul, where thousands of Koreans spend time every weekend on their knees with their open Bibles. As a result of all this fervor, believers and churches have multiplied, quickly changing the spiritual landscape.

Ten of the eleven largest megachurches in the world are in Seoul.[14] The largest Pentecostal church in the world (Dr. Cho's), the largest Presbyterian church, the largest Methodist church, and the largest Baptist church are all in this one city. I've had the privilege of speaking in each of these churches. I found their congregations filled with vital, praying, Bible-reading people. These are disciples who have a firm hold on The Book that tells people how to live.

The Most Wired Nation on Earth

Korea is not a sin-free utopia, but biblical influence has permeated every area of Korean society. In 1996 two former presidents were convicted of corruption. Why are these convictions remarkable? Because in earlier years, corruption was the norm for officials.[15]

Other signs of South Korea's healing are the great strides the nation has made in technology, education, and literacy. Whereas a bicycle was a luxury in 1971, South Koreans are now at the forefront of technology and manufacturing, exporting automobiles and electronics. In fact, Koreans use the Internet more per capita than any other country.[16] South Korea's push to get everyone online is part of a bigger picture—a commitment to making sure everyone gets an education. Recently Dr. Sek Yen Kim-Cho, a professor of linguistics at University at Buffalo, The State University of New York, told me that South Korea's illiteracy rate is only .002 percent.

When I heard about South Korea's remarkable literacy rate, I remembered all those underground believers. Through the years these believers kept the faith, and even the language, alive despite threats of imprisonment and death. They read God's Word using the script that a fifteenth-century Korean king invented after he received a message from heaven. The king's long view of how to help the Korean people and the faithfulness of generations of Korean believers led to the "overnight" success of the church and the country.

Chapter 10

Revolution
in a Tiny Land

Pitcairn

Releasing the Word of God and applying its principles will lift and bless any country because these principles are universal. They've been proven in country after country, small and large. When God takes hold of a person or a nation through his Word and by his Holy Spirit, the effect is revolutionary.

Early one morning on a beautiful August day in 1991, we dropped anchor off the tiny British territory of Pitcairn Island. To reach this remote outpost, we had sailed three days from the Gambier Islands of French Polynesia on one of YWAM's Marine Reach ships, the *Pacific Ruby*.

The islanders met our vessel with a longboat. We had come at their invitation. That's the only way visitors are allowed onto Pitcairn, with a population of just fifty-five in 1991 and an area of less than two square miles of land.

The island rises from the ocean with steep, sea-battered cliffs on all sides. Grateful that we had these smiling men to navigate for us, we jumped carefully down onto their boat, bobbing on the swells.

Then we zigzagged through the violent waves crashing on the rocks to reach their small dock.

As we climbed "The Hill of Difficulty," a steep path to their settlement, Adamstown, I felt delighted to be there. I knew this tiny country had a fascinating story.

A Hell of Their Own Making

Mutineers from the HMS *Bounty* settled this island more than two hundred years ago. In 1789 nine sailors protesting what they believed to be unjust conditions aboard the *Bounty* rebelled and took over the ship.[1] First, they fled to Tahiti. After making several stops in various islands, the nine mutineers persuaded, or outright abducted, various Polynesians—ending up with six additional men, eleven women, and one child.[2] Their leader, Fletcher Christian, had heard of an uninhabited island called Pitcairn's, which had been charted wrongly by hundreds of miles. The island was literally "off the map."

Survivors from this small group of desperate sailors and islanders were the ancestors of the smiling men who greeted us upon our arrival at Pitcairn.

After many days of sailing, the mutineers found the lonely island, a rocky outcropping in the emptiest part of the South Pacific. After dragging everything they could salvage up the steep hill—which they later named The Hill of Difficulty—the men took a desperate step. They knew the British would be scouring the seas to capture them and bring them to justice at the end of a hangman's noose. So they torched the *Bounty*, sinking it and making themselves castaways for life.[3]

The island had fresh water, and the men had brought animals from Tahiti and plants to grow for food. It shouldn't have been too bad living there, hidden away from the rest of the world. But after only a few years, life for the inhabitants of Pitcairn descended into a hell of their own making. One of the men discovered how to make liquor from the roots of the *ti* plant, which grew abundantly on the island. Soon his homemade still was producing enough alcohol to keep them all drunk. Fights broke out, usually over the women or racial slurs. Some of the castaways died of disease. One killed himself by plunging over the cliffs into the sea. No one knows for sure, because accounts differ, but at least two massacres took place. Finally, the Polynesian men and all of the mutineers were dead except for one—Alexander Smith, who renamed himself John Adams. Besides Smith/Adams, ten women survived, plus the offspring of the mutineers.

From Bedlam to The Book

What happened next changed the forlorn settlement drastically. Adams found a Bible in Fletcher Christian's sea chest—a Bible Fletcher's mother had tucked in before he left England. Adams began to study The Book. It wasn't long before he met the Writer and surrendered his life to God. Adams then taught the women and the young people what it said. And everything changed on Pitcairn Island.

Sir Charles Lucas, writing an introduction to Pitcairn's earliest history book, summed it up well:

> Many notable cases of religious conversion have been recorded in the history of Christianity, but it would be difficult to find an exact parallel to that of John Adams. The facts are quite clear. There is no question as to what he was and did after all his shipmates on the island had perished. He had no human guide or counselor to turn him into the ways of righteousness and to make him feel and shoulder responsibility for bringing up a group of boys and girls in the fear of God. He had a Bible and a Prayer Book to be the instruments of his endeavour, so far as education, or rather lack of education, served him. He may well have recalled to mind memories of his own childhood. But there can be only one simple and straightforward explanation of what took place, that it was the handiwork of the Almighty, whereby a sailor seasoned to crime came to himself in a far country and learnt and taught others to follow Christ.[4]

In 1808, an American ship, the *Topaz*, stumbled onto the uncharted island and found the settlement—Adams, the women, and the young people, some of them now in their late teens.[5] The captain and crew of the *Topaz*, as well as those from other ships that followed quickly over the next several years, described a happy, tranquil settlement.

For whatever reason, the initial hue and cry for the mutineers had died down. Two British captains finally came by Pitcairn while on other errands and returned to England with the recommendation that King George's government leave the Pitcairners alone. They said the culture on the island was like a Golden Age.[6] Since Adams had begun teaching them from the Bible, no young woman had been seduced. Theft was unknown. They lived in order and peace.[7]

That was nearly two hundred years ago. Now in 1991, we were allowed to visit the descendants of the mutineers and the Polynesian women. Over the years, many Pitcairners have moved to Norfolk Island, New Zealand, or elsewhere, looking for employment and room to raise their families. Much has changed, of course. Only about fifty remain on Pitcairn today.[8]

My family and I stayed with the pastor, and I preached in their tiny church. Our team, which included a doctor, two nurses, a dentist, and a dental assistant, gave the Pitcairners some much-needed medical help.

One of the biggest thrills was when they showed me the Bible taken from the *Bounty*.[9] They kept it in the church on a little wooden podium with a glass cover. They opened it for me, and I touched it carefully. As I held the aging leather-bound book in my hands, I thought of how God's Word had changed everything for those people long ago. I looked out the window and watched little children playing in the sunshine. I tried to imagine what it was like before the Bible changed Pitcairn from a place of drunkenness, murder, and suicide. I ran my fingers over the yellowing pages and thought what a difference The Book made in this, the smallest of countries.

Chapter 11

The Greatest Revolution of All Time: Martin Luther

Germany

It's easier to quickly see changes in a small country like Pitcairn. A small place is like a laboratory, where change can be seen clearly. But what about major nations? Can we see the same kind of impact from The Book? Yes, just this sort of thing happened in Germany in the 1500s.

In a part of Germany called Saxony, a young man named Martin Luther entered a monastery of Augustinian hermits, hoping to find forgiveness and salvation for his soul. But even though he strictly obeyed all their religious disciplines and more, he was acutely aware that he was lost. He tried desperately to find salvation through good works, all the while tormented with guilt. He felt that God was standing ready to condemn him. The leader of his order, John Staupitz, tried to encourage the young man. He told him the Lord was going to use him for great purposes. He said, "Let the study of the Scriptures be your favorite occupation."[1]

Devouring the Pages

During his second year at the monastery, Martin started reading the Bible in the monastery library. He began devouring the pages, asking God to make his Word plain to him.[2]

When the abbot sent him on an errand to the Vatican, Martin took the opportunity to do more penance, trying to find salvation at "the very gate of heaven," as Rome was called. He climbed the Holy Stairs in Rome on his knees as a faithful pilgrim, believing the promise that it would take fifteen years off his time in purgatory. Suddenly a scripture he had read came into his mind so strongly that he stood up. He felt it was God himself speaking to him: "The just shall live by faith!"[3] Christ wasn't offering him fifteen years' reprieve from purgatory. He was offering full and free salvation for eternity. It was a strong word, but still Martin lacked the assurance for his soul.

What he saw while in Rome shocked the young man. Sexual immorality and greed were rampant, and Luther reacted to priests who were cynical toward their sacred office.[4] Seeing how bad it was there at "the very gate of heaven" sowed the seeds for Luther's later call for the church to reform.

But first, he sought reformation in himself. He was ordained to the priesthood in 1507 and became a professor at the university in Wittenberg. He also served as local priest and confessor at the Castle Church. Even though he still struggled personally, his dedication to study made him a popular preacher and teacher.

Finally, in 1513, while preparing a lecture, he read about God's righteousness in Psalm 31:1. Thinking of God's righteousness always made him uneasy. Then Martin remembered Romans 1:17, where it speaks of God's righteousness and the power of salvation for every believer. Those words came back that he had heard so clearly while crawling up the Holy Stairs: "The just shall live by faith." It dawned on him that righteousness was a gift of God to be received simply by those who believed Christ died for them. Later he wrote, "When I realized this, I felt myself absolutely born again. The gates of paradise had been flung open and I had entered. There and then the whole of Scripture took on another look to me."[5]

The power of the Word and the Holy Spirit's work in his heart and mind reformed Martin Luther. Now Luther set about reforming those around him, preaching that salvation was a gift of God to be received by faith, not something to be earned. The stage was set for a confrontation that would split the church, change Europe, and eventually, change the whole world.

Selling Salvation

Realities bombarded Luther while he was serving as a local priest and confessor. He was able to see what common folk went through. He was particularly saddened and outraged when the church sold them indulgences.

An indulgence promised release from punishment after death for a person's sins. People could buy indulgences for themselves or for a deceased loved one in purgatory. One of the pope's powers was to give out these indulgences.

While Luther was serving in Wittenberg, the pope decided to really push the sale of indulgences as a fund-raiser. He was trying to finish building the glorious Saint Peter's Basilica. His representatives went out selling indulgences with the slogan, "When the coin in the coffer rings, the soul from purgatory springs."

When they came to his town, Luther was disturbed, to say the least. He saw his parishioners buying indulgences with money they needed to feed and house their families. It just wasn't right. He began to preach against the sale of indulgences, saying that God's gift of salvation had already been purchased by Christ on the cross.

Finally, in 1517, Luther wrote up a paper inviting debate. He wrote ninety-five of his propositions, or "theses," and according to custom, nailed them to the church door in Wittenberg.[6] Besides addressing the sale of indulgences, Luther's ninety-five theses dealt with repentance, the forgiveness of sin, and the greed and worldliness of the church hierarchy.

Luther intended to open an orderly, professional debate. Instead his paper set off a firestorm of controversy. The ninety-five theses were quickly translated from Latin into German and duplicated on a fairly new and incredibly important invention, the printing press.

In two weeks, the ninety-five theses spread throughout Germany. Within a month they were all around Europe.[7]

Most Important Work in Hiding

The church reacted immediately to this direct challenge to the pope's authority. It branded Luther a heretic and ordered him to appear in Rome to answer for his actions. If he had gone, he probably would have been killed, like other would-be reformers. Instead, a German prince intervened and spirited him away into hiding. While in seclusion Luther accomplished his most important work: he translated the Bible into German, the language of the people. Before this, the Bible had been in Latin, and only the elite could read it. Giving The Book back to the people was what would change Luther's nation and others. We'll see in the next chapter how his German Bible fueled one of the greatest revolutions of all time.

Luther didn't intend to leave the church. Like others before him, he wanted to bring it back to its foundational beliefs, to bring reformation. However, though both sides tried to make peace, the rupture was too severe. In a hearing before the pope's emissaries at the Diet of Worms in 1521, Luther refused to back down on his right to interpret the Word of God. He said, "I cannot and will not retract, for it is neither safe nor wise to do anything contrary to conscience. Here I stand, I can do no other. May God help me. Amen."[8]

The pope responded by excommunicating him. In a world where the church held power over an individual's salvation, that was the worst thing the pope could do to Luther. He was, in effect, condemning Luther to hell.

The Idea That Changed Everything

All of these events were far bigger than those involved realized. When Luther rejected papal authority, he was saying something important about the nature of the church itself. Most people thought "the church" was the religious establishment—particularly the bishops and the pope. Laymen were only passive members. They were dependent on the priesthood and subject to the teaching and ruling authority of the bishops.

It's hard for us to understand the control the institutional church had over people's lives. Bishops ruled like princes, taking on things we consider roles of the government today. For example, the pope could raise an army and wage war, and bishops could imprison people and execute them. The church even intimidated kings into submission.

When Luther challenged that exclusive authority, he was saying the church wasn't just the priests and bishops. It was all the people who believed in Christ—a "priesthood of believers." He and other Reformers found this idea of a kingdom of priests in both the Old and New Testaments—the understanding that God wanted to relate directly to his people and guide them.[9]

"The priesthood of all believers" was the central idea of the Reformation. Those who believed in Christ could come directly to God without depending on human authority or ceremony. Other New Testament passages, particularly Paul's words in Galatians 3:28, where he said there is neither Jew nor Greek, slave nor free, male nor female, reinforced the belief that all were equal before God. All are one in Christ Jesus.

So every person was free under God to search the Scriptures and live by his or her conscience. As Luther put it, "A Christian man is the most free lord of all and subject to none," and yet, "A Christian man is the most dutiful servant of all and subject to every one."[10] This truly revolutionary idea from God's Word would change not only Germany but nation after nation as the Reformation spread.

Chapter 12

Unlocking the Wealth

Germany (contd.)

The exciting new understanding of the priesthood of all believers began to reshape the church immediately. Many became "Protestants" and split away from Rome. Meanwhile, the Catholic Counter-Reformation started tackling some of the abuses in the church. It took centuries, but many of the things that shocked young Luther, such as the sale of indulgences, were dealt with. However, the split between Protestants and Catholics would lead to much violence and to wars that went on for centuries—even until recently in places such as Northern Ireland.

A few years ago, a Roman Catholic priest from Mexico City visited our mission in Kona, Hawaii. He was a true brother in the Lord. He had led revival meetings, emphasizing personal salvation and holiness, in more than eight hundred dioceses in various countries. When my sister Janice asked the Mexican priest what he thought of Martin Luther, I thought his answer was remarkable. He said, "God sent Martin Luther to call the church to repentance, but she didn't listen." Now in modern times, this priest from Mexico City was doing everything he could to call fellow Catholics to know Christ personally.

It took centuries for Protestants and Catholics to achieve even a tiny bit of cooperation. The initial violence unleashed during Luther's time was brutal. The bloodshed shocked Luther. But his teaching had lit a fuse that quickly spread beyond church walls. Over time, Reformation thought—and the Scriptures the Reformers embraced and shared with all the people—would contribute much to the radical reforming of society and even how people understood government. The Reformation and its by-products paved the way for democracy, for education of the common people, and for ideas of human rights. It ended with the greatest explosion of wealth and knowledge in the history of the world.

A Bible Everyone Could Read

With few exceptions, before the Reformation only scholars and educated priests studied the Bible. They would pass along its content to the ordinary people (or not) as they saw fit. In fact, many of the elite felt it was *dangerous* to let ordinary people read the Bible for themselves, that is, if they were able to read at all. The people might get wrong ideas about religion or, just as bad, question their rulers.

However, the Reformers believed that all people were equal before God and could come to him directly. Believers were part of the kingdom of priests. Therefore, they all needed to have the Word of God. How else could they know how God wanted them to live? Unfortunately the only Bible translation commonly available was Jerome's Latin translation, done in the fifth century. And no one but scholars and priests understood Latin anymore.

Translating the Bible into the language of the people and trying to distribute it was dangerous business. During the previous one hundred years in England, many people had paid with their lives or been driven into exile for their efforts to translate the Bible for the common people. And when they did succeed, the authorities confiscated and burned the Bibles.

Martin Luther, however, decided his people must have a Bible they could understand. His German Bible, completed while he was in hiding, put God's Word into the hands of the people. The importance of this one act can hardly be overstated. Luther's translation transformed the German language and empowered one of the most radically progressive movements of all time.

Earlier, something else had laid important groundwork for this revolution of hearts and minds fueled by the German Bible. In 1437, another German, Johannes Gutenberg, invented the printing press with movable type. Books would no longer be luxury items only for the elite. This technology was ready at just the right time to quickly spread Luther's new translation, as well as pamphlets and books with scriptural teaching.

My Asian friends point out that they had printing presses before Gutenberg. That may be true, but their presses did not lead to liberation and prosperity. The invention of the printing press together with the release of the Bible in the language of the people changed the face of Europe and, eventually, the world.

Unlocking the Wealth

Once the Bible was available in the people's language, another critical element in the revolution came into play. It wasn't enough to have the Bible in their language. The people also had to know how to read. The Reformers launched reading programs across Germany and much of Europe. And once people could read the Bible, they could also read other things—religious pamphlets, long narratives, poetry, political pamphlets and news, and books on everything from agriculture to bookkeeping to architecture—in other words, all kinds of useful information. Ideas could spread, and creative energies could be set free.

This changed all of history. Before this, there was no generally rich country on earth. Kings and tyrants were individually wealthy. A few aristocrats were wealthy. But not the common people. Individual potential exploded after the people were empowered by the concept of the priesthood of all believers. And as people learned to read, unprecedented numbers began to use their minds ever more broadly, coming up with ideas that created wealth and changed the lives of many. A middle class blossomed, and whole nations became wealthy *after* a significant number of people applied the Word of God in their lives.

The gaining of new knowledge began to pick up speed. For centuries Europe had actually lagged behind the Middle East and Far East in creative development. They forgot much of their inheritance from Greece and Rome, while the Islamic world happily absorbed it and built on it. The Arabs invented the numbers we all use and the concept of zero; the Chinese had many inventions before the West, including paper and gunpowder. But these innovations soon paled in comparison to bright, new discoveries coming out of Europe.

About one hundred years before Luther, Europeans had rediscovered Greek and Roman writings. A major rebirth of knowledge and exploration of new concepts known as the Renaissance took hold in Europe. The age of exploration also began, with Europeans pushing outward in ships to discover more about their world. And most important, they recovered knowledge of ancient languages, which opened a whole new study of Scripture.

However, as important as the Renaissance was to open people's minds and launch great works of literature and art, it was the Reformation that changed the lives of ordinary people. As more and more people learned to read, discoveries began to multiply exponentially in the West, eventually eclipsing the achievements of every other part of the world. Today our knowledge base doubles every three to five years. In just one field, biological science, knowledge doubles every 180 days.[1]

Sometimes leaders misunderstand the imbalance of technological expertise between Christian and non-Christian parts of the world. In the late 1990s, news reports told of the Chinese stealing nuclear secrets from the West. Chinese Premier Zhu Rongji denied the reports. I heard his remarks, translated and reported on CNN: "Don't you think we Chinese are as smart as you?"

Of course Chinese people are smart. There are smart and not-so-smart people in every country on earth. And since there are more Chinese on earth than any other nationality, there are more gifted Chinese. Intelligent people are born every day in India, Russia, and the Middle East. But how many Western young people go to China, India, Russia, or the Middle East to study science and technology? I don't say this as a point of competition or national pride. We need to consider this basic issue.

What causes the "brain drain" of scientists, doctors, and professional people? Why do these people leave their countries for places so different from their culture and religious beliefs? They are looking for freedom and the opportunity to realize their potential. After they arrive, they build their mosques and temples. They don't realize that the churches around them and the Bible are the sources for what they seek in their new country.

Mariano Grondona, professor of government at the Law Faculty of the National University of Buenos Aires, says that no country was a developed nation before the 1600s, neither in the East nor in the West: "It was the Protestant Reformation that first produced economic development in northern Europe and North America."[2] He adds that today the rate of economic growth in Protestant countries has declined in part because of the cooling of religious fervor.

We need to let all nations know that applying the truth and wisdom of God, the Creator and Sustainer of the universe, will enable them to flourish. Whether a nation is small and footloose like Pitcairn or large and deeply rooted like Germany, God has the power through his Spirit and his Word to do what seems impossible. Working with him, we can bring his blessings to every nation. Principles from God's Word are universal. They have been proven in country after country to bring about freedom and justice, a flourishing of creativity, and an increase in people's reaching their potential.

Chapter 13

John Calvin and
the Smelliest City
in Europe

Geneva

One of the best examples of how the Bible changed a country is the story of Switzerland.

This nation takes your breath away as you drive through it. Unblemished green countryside rolls by on both sides, framed by snow-covered mountains. Storybook chalets with gables and flower-filled window boxes nestle in valleys and perch on hillsides. As you drive farther, you approach solid, affluent cities with gardens, parks, great mansions, and boulevards lined with elegant shops filled with designer clothing and other luxuries.

It's tempting to think it has always been like this in the land of the solid red flag centered with a simple white cross. But Switzerland used to be terribly poor, always at the mercy of her more powerful neighbors. The reformation of Switzerland involved many people and places. But to understand the transformation in this region we can look at the story behind just one city, Geneva. One of our YWAM leaders, Dr. Tom Bloomer, has made an in-depth study of Swiss history, especially that of Geneva. I am indebted to

Tom and to Jim Stier for allowing me to share this story from their forthcoming book *Transformation for the Nations*.[1] They show how the worst of places became a shining example for the world. It is a remarkable story of transformation, rooted in the power of God's Word.

A City Transformed

Imagine we are visiting Geneva in the year 1530. The odor hits us first. Geneva has certainly earned its nickname, The Smelliest City in Europe. As we approach, we see crumbling city walls and streets strewn with garbage and human waste. The smells of vomit, sour wine, and urine pinch our noses. We hold our possessions tightly as we notice what sorts of people are crowding around us. We've already heard about the city's many criminals, political refugees, soldiers of fortune, spies, sailors from Lake Geneva, traders, prostitutes, and desperately poor slum dwellers. Now that we're here, we're glad we don't have to stay long in this pesthole.

You may be thinking that all cities of the Middle Ages were smelly and poor. True, but Geneva was especially so. And it was stunning how quickly the city changed.

From the Worst to the Best

How did such a terrible city become so prosperous? How did a place of crime and corruption become the crossroads of international diplomacy and a center for humanitarian agencies and international organizations? How did a place of great ignorance end up as the location of so many prestigious schools where the world's elite send their children to study? Why has Geneva become the place for enemy nations to meet and sign important treaties? How has this city and this nation remained free and without war for three centuries?

Of course, a full study of the history of Geneva and Switzerland reaches beyond the scope of this book. But if we want to understand the differences among nations, why some are poor and some are rich, surely we should pay close attention to Switzerland and, particularly, Geneva.

Geneva's transformation started with a man named John Calvin. Calvin was as important to the French Reformation as Martin Luther was to the German one. Calvin and other Reformers in the French-speaking world emphasized the need for personal salvation. They urged people to repent and trust God. But they didn't stop there. They immediately set out to teach people systematically, using their pulpits to reform society.

Teaching Free People How to Live

For centuries the church and nobles had been the only authority in Geneva. No one had to question what to do—it was determined for them. Geneva was an independent city-state. Its people were free, but who would tell them how to live? Calvin and his friends searched the Scriptures, teaching the people what God had to say about every area of life. Their goal was to build a city founded on God's Word, a city that could be a model for other cities throughout Europe.

Calvin preached sermons that emphasized individual responsibility and the value of work as worship. In the past, church thinkers had tended to separate the "sacred" from the "secular," teaching that only the church was holy, set apart from the unclean, profane things of everyday life. People were supposed to come to church for a sort of spiritual bath before plunging back into another week in the dirty world.

In contrast, the Reformers taught the people to wash their world with God's Word and with prayer. As Paul told Timothy in 1 Timothy 4:4–5, all of God's creation can be made holy. Calvin and the other Reformers viewed life holistically. Every job could be a calling from God. Worship was not just for Sunday. Work done with excellence the other six days was also worship "as working for the Lord."[2] The Reformers believed that God was sovereign over all of life, private and public. True disciples surrendered everything to God's guidance.

This and other ideas from the Reformers blazed across the continent. As soon as Calvin preached a sermon on Sunday, it was quickly printed in pamphlet form and carried all over Europe. These sermons touched on all sorts of areas.

The Reformers preached on what it meant to have a God-centered family. The men of Geneva were terrible fathers—dishonest, irresponsible, and often drunk. Disorder in the families was reflected in the poverty and immorality of the city. Now the Reformers emphasized taking care of their families, staying sober, working hard, paying their bills, giving their tithes, and saving for the future. In Geneva these teachings were also given the force of law, as the city council enacted the code Calvin presented to them.

When Max Weber, the German economist, was looking for the reasons for Western prosperity, he claimed it began in Geneva. In his book *The Protestant Ethic and the Spirit of Capitalism*, he gave credit to Calvin and his teachings in that city.[3]

John Calvin searched the Word of God for all sorts of economic principles; for example, he taught the bankers not to charge high interest, for that was the sin of usury. He fixed interest rates at 4 percent, high enough for the lender to make some money on his capital but low enough that the borrower could finance a new venture. Calvin's 4 percent interest rate lasted for four centuries in Switzerland.

All of this teaching had an immediate economic impact. Geneva and Switzerland began to prosper.

Chapter 14

Laying Foundations
for Freedom

Geneva (contd.)

Today, many people, including political leaders, believe there
is only a certain amount of wealth in this world. The policies they advocate assume that we must devise ways of dividing
limited resources into smaller and smaller portions. But the Bible
doesn't teach this. Redistribution of wealth never brings prosperity.
It only breeds more greed, corruption, injustice, and class envy. A
few powerful people grasp the resources while the poor and weak
sink farther down. The middle class disappears altogether. Lethargy
takes hold, replacing the joy and productivity of people taking
initiative.

The people of Switzerland and other countries of the Reformation discovered that there are no limits when free people use
biblical principles to create new wealth. Prosperity increases as
individuals are able to release their true, God-given potential.

Modern economists now have ideas in line with John Calvin,
who got his principles from The Book. They will tell you that any
country will prosper if it works hard, saves money, makes sure its

families stay intact, has reasonable interest rates, and lives under a system of law and accountability. The International Monetary Fund and the World Bank teach some of these principles to their member nations. But back in the sixteenth century, John Calvin got these ideas from the Bible.

Educating All God's Children

As part of his agreement with the city fathers to help reform Geneva, Calvin required that they build a school and put up the money to teach all the children—a truly revolutionary idea. Because each child was created in the image of God, the Reformers believed each child must be taught to read God's Word. For the first time in the history of the world (outside of ancient Israel), school was for every social class, not just the rich. And unlike in ancient Israel, even the girls were included this time.

Because of the Reformation, more and more people were able to read and study. This new literacy led to an explosion of knowledge. In prior centuries, only a small number of people were educated. What a terrible waste when you realize that God gives gifts to every child—talents and skills waiting to be released to bless everyone! When we deny freedom and the opportunity to read, we cut off the release of new inventions and ideas.

My wife, Darlene, and I went on a walking history tour of Geneva with Dr. Tom Bloomer. I was thrilled to stand in front of John Calvin's school, looking up at its sturdy stone walls. This was where it all began. I felt like we were standing at the headwaters of a great, mighty river of education that has flowed to millions upon millions of boys and girls.

Laying the Foundation for the Free World

Another concept that Calvin and the Reformers found in Scripture was the sinfulness of man. At first glance, this doesn't seem like a great idea to build society on. However, because of their awareness of this truth, that no human is perfect, the Reformers taught that the power of leaders and government should be limited. Their system of checks and balances was patterned after the separation of powers in the Old Testament. The Reformers aimed to keep rulers from having too much power, giving in to their sinful natures and becoming corrupt tyrants. The three-part government they devised with judicial, legislative, and executive branches came from the book of Deuteronomy and from Isaiah 33:22: "The LORD is our judge, the LORD is our lawgiver, the LORD is our king."

The Swiss Reformers went even further. They not only divided power among the three branches of government but also put each branch in a different city. And they separated power among the national level, the cantons (like states or provinces), and the towns.

Europe carefully watched this pilot project of using biblical principles to build a nation. Eventually the Geneva model would be copied and adapted by many countries, even centuries later by the framers of the United States Constitution with its executive, legislative, and judicial branches.

Freedom wasn't an accident that happened in Western Europe and North America. It grew out of the teachings of believers who sought the Word of God for principles of government. The Free World owes a singular debt of gratitude to John Calvin and other preachers of the Reformation.

Caring for the Poor

Swiss Reformers also saw in Scripture that they were responsible for the poor. In the 1500s, Geneva began to receive refugees as Protestants fled persecution from Catholic rulers in England, Scotland, France, and the city-states of Italy. In fact, the very word *refugee* was coined by these believers, based on the Old Testament concept of cities of refuge. Though this influx of foreigners could at times produce tension, the people of Geneva received these refugees into their homes. On our walking tour of Geneva with Dr. Bloomer, we stood on a hill overlooking rows of old buildings. Tom pointed out where, centuries later, you can still see the line of demarcation on the old buildings where the citizens of Geneva built new stories onto their homes to receive the refugees. What generosity and hospitality!

In time these refugees contributed a great deal to making Geneva the remarkable place it became. Many were artisans, musicians, and members of Europe's emerging business class. They brought new skills and much new knowledge to the city and, eventually, to the whole of Switzerland.

The Reformers formed an organization to care for newly arrived refugees and for widows and orphans. However, even the poor were considered to be responsible before God to improve themselves. Anyone who was able to work had to, even though he received help. The Geneva pattern of caring for the poor was copied and adapted throughout Europe, becoming the prototype for charities and reform movements for years to come.

Necessity Was *Not* the Mother of Invention

Academics teach that social changes happen because of great need, leading people who are change agents to seek a solution.

If that were true, why weren't orphanages and hospitals and all kinds of humanitarian agencies created in India or China, where the needs were the greatest? Necessity was not the mother of invention; the revelation of Scripture gave birth to these ideas. It has always been the Bible-informed heart that sees problems and works to meet the needs.

Calvin has his detractors, of course. His efforts to reform society weren't always consistent with Scripture. But he laid a solid foundation. The biblical principles he taught for social reform, education, government, and economics, particularly his ideas that all pursuits of life could be sacred, brought freedom and prosperity. His ideas spread to Scandinavia, Scotland, England, and Holland, and through the Puritans to the New World. Through the centuries, these nations and others have been profoundly influenced by this man who sought to build a city founded on God's Word.

The "En*dark*enment"

Sadly, the progress of Geneva itself would not always be upward. In following generations, the city—and indeed Western Europe—moved away from the biblical principles that led to their wealth and freedom. The Reformers' insistence on educating the public paved the way for an even greater explosion of scholarly pursuits. However, this evolved into a philosophical movement called the Enlightenment in the 1700s. It was based on rationalism—the idea that man by his own powers of reason could come up with any truth he needed.

Instead of looking for answers in God's Word, scholars turned to more humanistic sources, especially to the ideas of ancient Greece. The universities and seminaries of Geneva and the rest of Europe quickly filled with professors and students who knew nothing of God's revealed truth in the Bible. Rather than becoming enlightened, Europe was plunged into spiritual darkness. We can only wonder what would have happened if the Reformation had continued without this interruption. Would we have ended up with the bloody revolutions and terrible wars of the nineteenth century? If Europe's leaders had continued to search the Bible for principles to run their lives and countries, would we have seen the tragedies that burst out of Europe in the twentieth century— fascism under Hitler and Mussolini, and communism under Lenin and Stalin?

Turning the Light Back On

Through centuries of gathering darkness and ignorance of God's Word, the Lord still graciously worked to bring revival and correction. For a time, Geneva lost its freedom. At the beginning of the nineteenth century, the city-state came under the control of Napoleon. Finally, the people of Geneva regained their political freedom and joined the Swiss confederation in 1814.

Then in 1815, a young Scotsman named Robert Haldane came as a missionary to Geneva. He was appalled by how little the people knew of God and his Word. He started holding Bible classes. Many upper-class people became followers of Jesus. New churches were born, and they launched a missionary movement to French-speaking countries in Africa and the Pacific. People relearned crucial truths that had been taught by the Reformers.

While the scholars' pursuit of biblical understanding never again approached what it was during the Reformation, the people of Geneva and Switzerland still enjoyed what Francis Schaeffer called "the fruit of the fruit of the fruit" of godly forefathers. Their homeland continued to develop as a unique place in Europe— small, but prosperous and at peace with all.

Mercy to the Nations

Most people know that the International Red Cross makes its headquarters in Geneva. Not many know that the Red Cross came as a result of spiritual revival. The Red Cross began with a Swiss named Henri Dunant. As a young man, Dunant belonged to a church started during Haldane's revival meetings. While he was still a teenager, he began meeting with other young men to study the Bible and find ways to help the poor.[1] Later as Dunant was traveling, seeking to make his fortune in the world, he came upon the site of a gruesome battle between the French and Austrian armies in a place called Solferino. He saw the bodies of the wounded and dying scattered across the field. He asked why no one was helping them. People told him to ignore the casualties, to go on his way and not worry. They explained that if he tried to go out and help the wounded, one or both sides of the conflict would shoot at him. This had always been the way of wars and battles—the wounded had to either get themselves up and away or lie there and die.

Dunant believed this was wrong. It wasn't according to the ways of God that he had learned in his home church in Geneva. In 1862, he wrote a pamphlet called *A Memory of Solferino*. This leaflet was printed and reprinted until thousands of people across Europe had read it. It roused the consciences of people everywhere. As a result, Dunant was invited to speak before kings and parliaments about the treatment of wounded soldiers. Dunant's efforts led to the Committee of Five, a forerunner of the International Red Cross. The following year, this committee hosted the first Geneva Convention in October of 1863, with sixteen nations signing a treaty that defined the rights of the wounded and limited other horrors of war. The document was based on principles from the book of Amos, showing God's concern for the just conduct of war and righteous treatment of prisoners.

Thus the reformation of Geneva and Switzerland, first undertaken by Calvin and other Reformers, spilled over into the larger world, influencing nations with God's justice, righteousness, and mercy.

You Can Be a Nation Builder

Certainly, by any definition Calvin, Luther, Hauge, Kuyper, Carey, and Wesley were nation builders. You, too, can be a nation builder by obeying Jesus and applying his Word in any one of the seven spheres that influence society. Are you making Jesus lord in your profession? Are you searching through the Bible to find principles and practices relevant to your occupation? If you are a pastor or a leader of a ministry, are you encouraging your people to do this? Are you bringing the kingdom of God into your workplace, modeling godly behavior and exercising your influence with quiet strength?

These examples of nation builders may seem daunting. They certainly make my efforts seem small in comparison. You might not be able to ski with Bibles or ride horseback for hundreds of thousands of miles to preach like Hauge or Wesley. You might not be able to influence all seven spheres of society like Carey or become a preacher/journalist/educator/politician like Kuyper. But could you choose eleven people to mentor according to the ways of Jesus and the Bible…in your lifetime? Surely that's a goal we could all work toward.

That's what Jesus did. He taught the multitudes, but the number of his serious followers fell to five hundred,[2] then withered away to only one hundred twenty.[3] He funneled his greatest efforts into training twelve, and he lost one of them. But look at what his eleven disciples did!

Jesus could have used his powers as the Son of God to launch an extensive program of mass education, training millions of followers. Instead, he showed us that discipleship is an up-close, personal thing. He invested himself in a few. He left us a pattern we can all aspire to. Everyone could train eleven people, living out God's principles before them. As our nations reap the fruit of the fruit of our fruit, we can all be regarded as nation builders.

Part 3

Transforming Truths
from God's Book

Chapter 15

The Key:
Who God Is

What is it about God's Book that transforms people and nations? I was privileged to hear Dr. Francis Schaeffer address this question when he visited our YWAM school in Switzerland in the late sixties. Dr. Schaeffer, the founder of L'Abri Fellowship, was a brilliant thinker.[1] He understood that Christianity is not only a religion but also the truth. The Bible is not true *because* we believe it; it is the truth *whether or not* we believe it. What I gleaned from Dr. Schaeffer's teaching were four basic ideas from the Bible that can make a huge difference in the way we view the world and in the way we live:

- Who God is
- Who man is
- The existence of unchanging, knowable truth
- The responsibility of man to live according to the truth

No matter what area of life you consider—whether it be grappling with great problems like human rights abuses and poverty, looking for how to ensure every child has an education, or seeking equal protection under the law for every individual—if you start with these four ideas you will end up with transformation.

While teaching at our school, Dr. Schaeffer said that these four truths are found throughout the Bible. However, he said that if all you had were the first six chapters of the Bible, you could still come up with these four ideas.[2]

We'll look at these four concepts individually, for these are the great ideas that bring blessing to people of The Book. In this chapter we'll touch on the first, foundational truth: who God is.

Knowing the character and nature of God changes us and our nations. God has extraordinary characteristics that we can build our lives and our society upon. It isn't my aim in this book to go into all the aspects of who God is. God is love and therefore just, kind, good, merciful, and much, much more. On such a vast topic, I'll focus on only two of the transforming truths about God.

Who God Is: Unity and Diversity

The biblical doctrine of the Trinity, God in three persons, is central to transforming nations. In the first chapter of Genesis, the name for God is *Elohim*. This is neither a singular nor a plural noun, but a compound unity, like a bunch of grapes. God is one, but he is also three persons. In Genesis 1:26, God says, "Let *us* make man in *our* image" (emphasis added).

This theme of God being one yet in three persons develops throughout the Bible. It teaches us a very important idea that will transform nations. That idea is unity and diversity—the basis for freedom in the political arena, for entrepreneurial spirit in the economic realm, and the underlying framework for universities in the academic world. Even the word *university* reflects this understanding—unified yet diverse. *Uni-versity.*

This idea of unity and diversity as displayed in the Trinity supports healthy relationships of all kinds. Yet it is an idea that finite man could never have come up with. God had to reveal it to us in Scripture. And still we can't fully grasp the Trinity. The best we can do is use illustrations, such as Saint Patrick did while preaching to the Celts. He showed them a shamrock with its three-part leaves—it is three, but it's one. It's unified, yet it has diversity built in.

Trinity metaphors fill the world. The earth is land, sea, and sky. Science deals with gas, liquids, and solids. We have ice, water, and steam. We measure in length, depth, and breadth. Time includes past, present, and future. Human beings are body, soul, and spirit. We could fill many pages with such examples. It seems that God has stamped his three-part nature into all of reality.

These illustrations help us, but we still can't fully explain the Trinity—God's simultaneous unity and diversity. It's not a problem of logic, either. The problem is, our minds are simply not adequate to explain an infinite God. C. S. Lewis said that our difficulty grasping the Trinity is like trying to imagine a cube if we lived in a two-dimensional world.[3]

Because countries with a church heritage have an understanding, albeit limited, of the Trinity, they are better equipped to handle the complexities of modern life, balancing freedom and order. They are blessed by the concept of unity and diversity. Even those who do not believe in God or the Bible benefit from living in a society based on this idea. For instance, in Europe many have departed from active faith in the triune God. But they are still enjoying the benefits from earlier generations' faith. They enjoy such things as democratic governments with separation of powers, personal freedom, ethnic pluralism, and productivity in their economies. They continue enjoying these blessings because of what believers built into their foundations centuries ago. That's why Western Europe is far different from other lands, where these foundations are missing. It's important to note, however, that these blessings will erode as people stray further and further away from biblical values. They will lose all the benefits, including those that come from understanding unity and diversity.

A few years ago, I was speaking in a Central Asian mosque to some Muslim leaders. I had become friends with the head of the mosque, who invited me to tell his colleagues what I believed about Jesus. Afterward these devout men had the usual objections. One said, "You believe in three gods!"

"No," I quickly replied, "there is only one God, but he is infinite. Any explanation I could give would be limited. But I can show you God's unity and diversity by my relationships. I am a son. I am also a father and a husband. Am I one person or three?" Then

I did my best to explain the mysterious relationship among God the Father, God the Son, and God the Holy Spirit.

It did not surprise me that these men at the mosque balked at one God in three persons. Only the God of the Bible is unified yet diverse. Most Muslims believe in one god in one person—unity without diversity. Hindus on the other hand have literally millions of gods—diversity to the max. A modern Hindu might assert that these are all expressions of one overall being, but it is so impersonal—sometimes defined just as "is-ness"—that there is no practical unity. Only the God of the Bible is both unity and diversity.

As humans, we can experience unity at the finite level, like in a loving marriage. And even then it's hard to describe how two people become one. But think of the infinite unity of the three personalities of God. We cannot define it completely, yet that doesn't mean it's not true. Think about just one aspect of their unity—their omniscience. God the Father, God the Son, and God the Holy Spirit are all infinite in their knowledge; they know all things. Nothing is hidden between them or from them. Imagine the potential for unity there. Also, all three have all power—omnipotence. Yet they are committed to the same purposes, and they cooperate to achieve their goals, deferring to one another in respect and total love. And all three can be present anywhere—omnipresence. In this and in every other way, God is moving in total unity yet with a richness of diversity we can't even imagine. With God, the unity and the diversity are both absolute. This blend allows for the greatest amount of creativity.

We Become Like the God We Worship

If you want to understand the Middle East, South Asia, or any other part of the world, you must understand the people's beliefs about their god. We all become like the god we worship, a little more each day, each year, each century.

Take most people in the Middle East and North Africa. They expect to be ruled from the top down, their society governed by religious legalism and rules strictly enforced by the government. Corruption of leaders is a way of life. No diversity of thought or action is allowed. When you worship their god—the ultimate portrayal of unity without diversity—you will reproduce the Middle

East and North Africa. It will even influence the environment. On one of my visits to Israel, I was admiring the people's diligent tree planting that made the desert bloom again. An expatriate living there told me of an earlier time when the Turks ruled in Palestine. The Turks taxed the people by counting their trees, so the people cut down their trees, and the desert grew. The dry harshness of the land soon mirrored the people's worldview.

If you want to live in a country with great problems of poverty and injustice, where the majority of the people are not free, worship Hindu gods. There you have the tyranny of diversity without unity. The freedom of the elite in India is held in place by a strict caste system, condemning millions to a miserable life without opportunity. There is no basis for unity—their worldview is untempered by any belief in a moral God who creates all humanity in his image. Terrible suffering is kept in place because religious teachers say the unhappy multitudes are simply reaping judgment for evil works they committed in an earlier life. Brahmins, the top caste, make up only 5 percent of the population, but they hold 70 percent of the top government jobs and 78 percent of all judicial positions.[4] Missionaries in India tell me that most of India's wealth is controlled by only five families.

These sad worldviews should instill in us a desire to make sure we and our children worship the true God of the universe, the God revealed in Scripture. Only the God of the Bible is worthy of our worship. Only by worshiping him do we end up with free, prosperous countries where the majority of the people benefit.

Chapter 16

Your Beliefs
about God Matter

Any nation that does not have the concept of unity and diversity demonstrated in the Trinity doesn't have the same degree of freedom and creativity as nations that embrace the concept. It doesn't experience the explosion of knowledge and wealth unleashed when people fulfill their potential. Leaders need to understand unity and diversity. It takes many kinds of people doing different kinds of work, contributing their best ideas and efforts to create the most productive, prosperous society. If leaders don't value creative differences in people, their nation will miss out on what it can achieve.

Leaders may even try to force everyone into a single mold, thinking and acting alike, as in the dictatorships of the Soviet Union and Nazi Germany, or in modern totalitarian states such as Cuba and North Korea. History shows that such nations stagnate and eventually just collapse. There must be diversity for a healthy, productive whole, whether we are talking about nature, government, family, commerce, or any other arena of life.

Nabil, an Egyptian friend of mine, overheard three Arabs talking as they watched airplanes taking off in Kuwait. One of them said, "Why is it we can fly those jets but we can never create one?"

A good question. Why isn't wonderful technology flowing from Middle Eastern nations? Those nations have as many intelligent, gifted people per capita as any others in the world. But their worldview has hobbled their people with concrete thinking, legalism, and a rigid hierarchy—qualities that prevent a rise to world leadership. Their worldview hinders the progress of Middle Eastern culture and keeps people from developing innovative ideas.

Toppling Other People's Towers

Radical terrorists such as those in al-Qaeda or the Taliban are striving to return to what they consider a "pure" form of their religion, a form that will enable them to control people. Look at their attack on the World Trade Center and the Pentagon on September 11, 2001. They were like toddlers who couldn't build a tower of blocks themselves. So they knocked over what others had built. Extremists like these want to take the world back to a simpler time, such as the ninth century, a period when despots ruled. Their religion was able to undergird these rulers, who had absolute power and determined the agenda for everyone. If the ruler was benevolent, people could develop in a limited way. If he was a tyrant, people suffered greatly. Either way, a true release of creativity and ideas was cut off.

At one time, during Europe's Dark Ages, Muslim cities were centers for education and artistic achievements. But because of the rigidity inherent in their view of the world, they stagnated and lost their leadership. Modern development passed them by and still does today.

Diversity without Unity Leads to Chaos

Diversity without unity also leads to problems. Without unity we sink into anarchy. I have been to countries where diversity has run amok and all order has collapsed. It's a scary thing. I remember one country in central Africa where I saw soldiers robbing people at gunpoint. In another country I visited, warring factions controlled different parts of the city. It was utter chaos and no one was safe. These countries had diversity but no unity. It takes a blend of both unity and diversity for countries to be productive and free.

The Church in the East

Even civilizations that have a church heritage but lack understanding of the unity and diversity of the Trinity are limiting their potential. Take Russia, for example. Russia went from the strict rule of the czars to the even harsher rule of the communists. The nation developed in a very limited way under the czars. And after only seventy years of communism, its national wealth and strength were spent. Oppressive, hierarchical leadership bankrupted the creativity and initiative of the Russian people. They are still struggling to recover.

It's very important to learn from the past. These are not just dead, dry historical facts. What people believe about God affects their personal lives and their nations—it can determine whether or not they are able to fulfill their destiny. If we want to unleash the creativity of the East now, we need to understand what happened back then, especially what happened in the realm of ideas.

Fifteen hundred years ago, a split began in Christianity over the issue of a "hierarchy" in the Trinity.[1] This and other issues eventually led to the Great Schism between the Eastern and Western churches in the eleventh century. The Eastern church said God the Son and God the Holy Spirit are subordinate to God the Father. The Western church, on the other hand, held that each member of the Trinity is equal. The Father, Son, and Holy Spirit are continually submitting to one another in love.[2] This Western view allowed people to see that the Godhead, with absolute equality, has infinite unity *and* diversity.[3]

Creative Freedom and Blend

I know good brothers and sisters in the Lord who worship the Savior in Eastern Orthodox churches. Many Eastern saints have led lives of humble devotion and incredible faithfulness to Christ, standing firm against tyrants of all kinds. But in my opinion, the Eastern church's hierarchical view of the Trinity has led to serious problems for nations of the East. These nations didn't have the model of creative freedom and blend—the unity and diversity in God the Father, God the Son, and God the Holy Spirit. Because they didn't see mutual submission within the Trinity, Eastern believers lacked this pattern to develop nations of free, diverse yet unified people. They didn't have their own Reformation with an Eastern version of "the priesthood of all believers" releasing social, political, and economic benefits. Instead, their view of a hierarchy within the Trinity stifled development. Rather than people being free and releasing one another to use their gifts, they duplicated this hierarchical view of God at all levels of their society, from home life to government. Nations of the East went from the tyranny of absolute rulers to the crushing domination of Marxism, ending up in a political and economic implosion at the end of the twentieth century.

This kind of thinking isn't restricted to the East, either. I admit this temptation to a hierarchy mentality is in the West too. Plenty of people in the West have embraced this rigidity of leadership, which always cripples individual freedom. I've seen pastors and leaders of organizations who act like little kings, ruling over subservient people whose gifts are never released. We all need to remember and practice the principles of mutual submission and servant leadership.[4]

The Orthodox view of the Trinity made the churches of the East more vulnerable to this danger. God wants to release the individual gifts and talents of millions of Eastern Europeans and Russians. Those called to serve these peoples can help them rebuild their nations and economies by teaching them the unity and diversity modeled in the Trinity, along with servant leadership and mutual submission.

Undermining What They Came For

The West was able to develop, on the foundations of a triune God, the best expression of unity with diversity. This led to the freedom and prosperity we enjoy today. The rest of the world wants to come and enjoy it with us. I don't blame them. If I were a Hindu, I would want my children to come to the West to have a better life. We welcome them to the West, too, because we understand the value of diversity within unity. However, when Hindus, Buddhists, or Muslims build their temples and mosques and start to spread their teachings in the West—which they have the legal right to do in a free society—they are undermining the very things they came here to find.

God himself has set the example for us, modeling unity and diversity, submission and servanthood, in his very being and in dramatic form through the life of Jesus. We are supposed to follow his example. As we move into our potential and release others to do the same, all the while submitting to Christ and to one another, we will see creativity on an unprecedented scale. It's described for us in 1 Corinthians 12. This is dynamic creativity in an atmosphere of love and honoring one another. We will see answers to chronic problems released; we will see development we've never imagined. Nations will be transformed.

Who God Is: Infinite and Personal

We also learn in the first chapters of Genesis that God is infinite yet personal. And this fact—that God is both infinite and personal—is unique to the God of The Book.

Just as it is hard for us to grasp the concept of the Trinity, it is hard for us to fathom what it means to be infinite. God had no beginning and will have no end.[5] We can't understand that. Neither can we wrap our minds around his being all powerful and all knowing or grasp what it means for all things to be in his presence. We can see some of this in the first chapters of Genesis as he creates everything that exists by merely speaking. That astounds us.

However, when we see God relating to the humans he created on a personal level—that is when our hearts are warmed and wowed. As Dr. Schaeffer said, if all we had were the first few chapters of Genesis, we could see God's personal nature. God has intellect, will, and emotions. He thought of what he wanted to do, he chose to do it, and he had emotional reactions—first, joy and satisfaction with all he had created, then sadness when humans rebelled. We will see more about this in the next chapter as we see how God made man and woman in his image. Genesis, God's first revelation of himself, shows us he is both infinite and personal—a foundational truth with huge implications for how we live.

Only the God of the Bible

No other religion can make the claims that the Bible makes about God.

In the early 1970s, I met with a group of undergraduate and graduate theology students at Trinity College in Cambridge University. A few of their professors crowded in with us in a back room of their chapel. My audience that day was congenial and astute, yet I knew many of these seminarians didn't believe in God or the Bible. I decided to speak to them about how to prove there is a God.

I said, "Only those who worship the God of the Bible have a God who is both infinite and personal."

Then I waited. Some in the audience were experts on comparative religions. If I were to be bombarded, it would happen after that bold statement. But no one said anything. There was only silent acquiescence. The God of the Bible stands alone, unique among all the deities humans worship.

Think about it. Muslims pray five times a day. They say their god is great. They say their god is infinite. But they do not say their god came down and spoke to them. That would be blasphemy, because it's too personal. In my visits to every country, I have met good, devout Muslims. But I have never met one who speaks of a personal relationship with Allah.

Hinduism does not have a god who is both infinite and personal either. Hindus have Brahma, a god without limits who is impersonal. They cannot know him. They also have many finite personal gods. Some say there are 36 million gods in India; other sources say there are 330 million personal gods.[6] But Hindus have no infinite, personal God like the God of the Bible. They are like the Greeks whom Paul spoke to on Mars Hill—religious people with many gods. The God unknown to ancient Greeks and modern Hindus is the personal, infinite God of the Bible.[7]

Whatever religion you name—Buddhism, Taoism, Shintoism, animism, New Age—it is the same. Their god is either infinite and impersonal, finite and personal, or finite and impersonal. For some, there really isn't a god at all, just principles of being, or the universe.

Why does this matter? Because people become like the god they worship. Only the God of the Bible is worthy of our worship.

As we worship him, we build a free and prosperous society, formed around our love for God and others. Because the God of the Bible is infinite, we can trust him for creativity, development, and revelation beyond limits. And because the God of the Bible is personal, we can have meaning, relationships, and love in our lives. God's Word says we love because he first loved us.[8]

What we believe about God colors everything we do—in business, in government, in the media, in the arts, in our families, in our churches, and in the way we train our young. This foundation will determine our destinies as individuals and as nations. And because we were created in God's image, and because we have his Word to guide us, we can live the way he created us to live. We'll experience the greatest individual satisfaction, and we'll help create the healthiest, most productive societies.

There's so much more to say about who God is as revealed in Scripture. However, this book isn't an exhaustive treatment on the nature and character of God. It wouldn't be possible to list all he is revealed to be in Scripture and show all the blessings we have received through these foundational understandings. In this book I want to give you a taste. I want to make you hungry to search the Word of God for yourself, to dig into its treasures.

Dr. Schaeffer taught us three other biblical truths that transform nations. We'll look at these nation-changing ideas in the next chapters.

Chapter 17

Key Truths about Us

Nations with a Bible heritage have a better way of life. Nations without the Bible flounder and self-destruct. We've seen that God's Word is true whether or not we believe it. When we apply the truths of Scripture, we are living according to reality. When we do not have God's Word, or when we reject it, we are living unrealistically—without the wisdom of the Creator and Sustainer of the universe.

That's the big picture. We already looked at the first foundational truth: who God is. Now let's examine three other principles Dr. Schaeffer taught us.

Created in the Image of God

The first chapters of Genesis show God deciding to create human beings in his image.[1] God is personal and he made us as personal beings—each man and woman is created as a unique individual.[2] Like him, we each have the power to think and to feel and the ability to choose.

Because we are personal beings, each of us can have a personal relationship with our Creator. Six billion individuals can each have a personal relationship with him at the same time because he is both personal and infinite. What a fantastic privilege! Those who come to know him by accepting his Son, Jesus Christ, will live through all eternity being thrilled and stretched, learning more and more, loving him and receiving his love.

It might sound obvious to say we are personal, individual beings, but this idea is foreign to some. Eastern religions, such as Buddhism, teach that there are no individual people. Instead we are all part of one another, part of a great, impersonal life force.

After the Asian tsunami in December of 2004, various religious leaders tried to help people understand the tragedy. One account told of a Buddhist leader who tried to comfort those who had lost loved ones. The leader reminded them that all of life is an illusion. They shouldn't have allowed themselves to become so attached to their family members.

That's not the teaching of the Bible. According to God's Word, we are each unique and have tremendous value because we are made in the image of God. Jesus stood at the tomb of his friend Lazarus and wept.[3] Why did he cry when he was about to raise him from the dead? Perhaps Jesus was weeping over every individual who has died tragically, another casualty in a sinful world. Every individual counts. Every person has immeasurable worth. Knowing this makes a difference in how we treat others. It's the foundation for human rights. Because we are personal, we can relate to one another in a meaningful way. And because God loves us, we have the capacity to love others.

Created Higher Than the Animals

When you read the Genesis 1 account of Creation, observe the definite shift between verse 25 and verse 26. First, God makes all of nature—the land, the seas, the plants, and the animals. Then in verse 26, God comes up with a separate idea, another kind of creation. He says, "Let us make man in our image." He does that, making them male and female. Then he gives them the job of ruling over all of nature.

This is who we are. A special creation. We share much of our biology with animals, but the Word of God makes it clear we are also separate from them, distinct. For we are made in the image of God. When people don't have this biblical understanding, priorities become skewed and great harm is done.

A Temple for Rats

Some years ago I was talking with the CEO of a Fortune 500 company who had just returned from India. He wanted to do something for the people there, but he said, "I don't see how we can ever help them." Why did he say this? Because of the Hindu worldview.

For instance, when I first visited Calcutta, India, I was amazed to learn that the people would not kill rats. Instead of killing them, animal control workers would capture rats and set them free a few miles down the road. Their worldview elevates the vermin to a status equal to humans, even though the rats spread disease, destroy crops needed to feed starving people, and increase suffering.

In fact, sometimes Hindus seem to regard rats as more important than humans. The Karni Mata Temple in Deshnok is dedicated to the worship of rats. People lay out sugar and coconut in bowls on the floor for them. Can there be a worse example of wrong priorities than to set out delicacies for rats while millions in India go to bed hungry every night?

Hindus also consider the cow sacred, calling it "our mother." A friend in India told me that in her city the driver's test asks: "If you had a choice between hitting a human and hitting a cow, which would you hit?" People who answer that they would hit the cow can't get a driver's license in that city.

Strict Hindus are afraid to kill any animal because of their belief in reincarnation. They see animals as creatures on the same plane of interrelated life as themselves—as the present lives of "souls" once human but now reincarnated as rats or cows. If they kill these, they might be killing one of their own dead relatives now in animal form. Yet human suffering goes unrelieved because people don't know the supreme value of each individual created in the image of God.

Cruel neglect comes out of false understandings of the origin and destiny of men and women. Some Hindu teachers even criticized the work of Mother Teresa. They said she worked against the will of God by not allowing people to suffer. They believe people's suffering is caused by evil done in their previous lives. Now they have to atone for their sins. In their view, Mother Teresa's kindness merely prolonged a person's suffering in future reincarnations.

A biblical worldview would release the great potential of the Indian people. It matters what people believe. Justice, prosperity, and well-being come or are lost because of beliefs.

Created in the Image of God, but Limited

Even though we were created in God's image, we are not gods. We will always be finite because we were created. We will be finite even in heaven because each of us had a beginning. Neither will we know all things as God does. For God's Word says, "As the heavens are higher than the earth, so are my ways higher than your ways and my thoughts than your thoughts."[4] We will spend all eternity learning new things.

Man Is Flawed but Can Be Redeemed

We also see in Genesis that the first humans were created perfect and enjoyed friendship with each other and with God. The Lord kept a daily appointment with them, walking and talking, up close and personal. Despite this, Adam and Eve sinned by eating the fruit of the one tree God asked them not to eat from. Yet even then, God didn't abandon them. He explained what they had done and what the consequences would be. And before this tragic story concluded in chapter 3, God promised a Savior to rescue them and their descendants.[5]

That salvation briefly glimpsed in Genesis becomes more and more evident throughout the Old Testament until it is finally fulfilled with Jesus coming to earth, living, dying on the cross, and rising again—all to make us new again—clean, forgiven, and ready to do God's work.

Created for Meaningful Work

God designed us to find excitement and fulfillment in our work. This is another way that we are made in his image. The Creator God made us to be "creators with a small *c*." Our creativity is finite, whereas his is infinite. But he gives us true freedom to create. We can come up with new ideas and create things that never existed before.

This was true in the garden, before Adam sinned. God gave him the creative assignment of naming the animals. What a fun job that was! Imagine it—you're the first human being to ever see an elephant. What would *you* call it?

God still wants us to be creative. As we become his children through faith in Christ, he promises that the Holy Spirit will guide us in all things.[6] We shouldn't restrict the Holy Spirit's work in us, limiting him only to religious matters.[7] He wants to enable us to be creative, as he is, bringing innovation into every area of life.

He has plans for us that are far beyond our imagination.[8] God wants to create his kingdom on earth through us. Of course he wants to use us to bring people into reconciliation with him. But he also wants us to bring out new products and processes to bless everyone. He wants his people to discover cures for diseases and create all kinds of art that lift the human spirit. He even wants his people to find new ways of creating wealth, to provide jobs and make life better for everyone. Every good and perfect gift comes from God.[9] And there are no limits to what people can do in cooperation with their Creator.

Chapter 18

Truth Exists,
and You Can Know It

The existence of absolute truth is the third nation-changing principle from the early chapters of Genesis. The most basic truth is shown in the very first verse: *In the beginning God.* Every other absolute truth comes from that one: *God is.* And in the beginning God created. He created not only things but also laws and principles and truths. There is such a thing as truth because God created it.

The "Real" Facts

On the classic TV cop show *Dragnet*, Sgt. Joe Friday used to deadpan, "Give me the facts, ma'am. Just the facts." To solve his case, the detective didn't need opinion, pointless detail, or emotional outbursts. He just wanted the facts—exactly what happened and how. In other words, he needed the *essential* truth.

We have the same need in our lives. We need to know the truth.

We are surrounded by countless versions of "truth," some presented in a pretty compelling way. We often hear something like

"Everybody knows this is how you have to do things" or "This is how life really works." We see popular images of the successful life, examples we're supposed to model our lives on. Experts and leaders tell us how to solve our problems and what our nations need to do—usually disagreeing with one another. In fact, their own messages and opinions shift constantly.

We need to know what is *really* true, the truth that we can stake our lives on. Dr. Schaeffer was saying there is such truth—truth that is absolutely and always true—and we can know it. Absolute truth is a fixed point of reference, a "presupposition" of the entire Bible.[1]

How do we know what is true? Because of who God is. He is truthful, and he reveals truth to us. He does this by several means: through nature, through the moral law written on our hearts, through the Bible, and through his ultimate revelation, Jesus.

We know the truth because God has revealed it in his creation, in nature.

Paul told us this in the first chapter of Romans.[2] When we look at nature we learn much about the Creator. We see that he loves beauty and order and that he is unimaginably great and powerful. We find he is lavish and loves diversity. We can even see God's compassion, unselfish love, and faithfulness reflected in the behavior of certain animals. For example, I was so moved watching a French-made documentary called *The March of the Penguins.* The movie shows the sacrificial care of a father penguin for his offspring in Antarctica. The father penguin nearly starves while sheltering his offspring for months in blizzards, in howling winds up to one hundred miles an hour, and in temperatures as low as eighty degrees below zero Fahrenheit. When we see an example like that in nature, we learn a little about who God is, the One who created penguins.

We know the truth because God has written the moral law on our hearts and has given us a conscience that convicts us of right and wrong.

No one had to tell Adam and Eve they had done wrong when they ate from the forbidden tree. For the first time they felt shame and guilt. When God came to walk with them, they hid.

Paul said in Romans 2:14–15, that even those who have never heard God's Word still have God's law written on their hearts. Their conscience tells them when they do right and when they do wrong.

I have visited with people in every country on earth. I have seen that ideas of love, responsibility, right and wrong, conscience, and moral law exist in every culture. Every language has words for right and wrong, even before any contact with civilization or the Bible.

We know the truth because God has revealed himself to man throughout history and ultimately through Jesus Christ.

The Bible is a witness to these revelations. Paul said that all Scripture is inspired by God.[3] It is that outside reference point we all need to show us the way. The Bible is *God-breathed*, given to teach us, reprove us, correct and train us in righteousness.[4] The Lord promises that heaven and earth will pass away, but not his Word.[5]

The Bible isn't vague or uncertain when it comes to absolute truth. It gives us absolutes. However, not everything repeated in God's Word is a principle of absolute truth. For example, the Bible records the words of Satan with his evil pride and distortions. Our absolute point of reference is God himself, who inspired the Scriptures. The Bible is true because its Author is absolutely truthful. He is, in fact, the very definition of what is true, or real.

Jesus said in John 14:6, "I am the way and the truth and the life." He *is* the truth. Remember when Jesus stood before Pontius Pilate? He tells Pilate that he came into the world to show people the truth. Whoever wants truth will listen to him.[6] What a sad irony follows in the story. Pilate looks at Jesus, the embodiment of truth, and asks, "What is truth?" We have no record that Pilate ever found it.

Truth to Live By

God's Word reveals not only the facts about God but also the truth we need to know about ourselves: "For the word of God is living and active. Sharper than any double-edged sword, it penetrates even to dividing soul and spirit, joints and marrow; it judges the thoughts and attitudes of the heart."[7]

His Word gives us the way to live our lives. If you meditate on God's Word, you will prosper.[8]

This reminds me of a young Mexican boy in my parents' church years ago. His name was Frank Yubeta. Frank came from the humblest background. It was the middle of the Depression, and my parents were struggling to start a church in Somerton, Arizona—a speck of a town on the Mexican border. As a teenager, Frank helped my parents build a church out of adobe bricks they made themselves.

Later, Frank and his new bride, Viola, moved to the West Coast. They owned very little, but after World War II, Frank began building houses out of reclaimed lumber. By the end of their lives they had built a successful retail plumbing business in Oxnard, California, while supporting many missionaries and organizations. Their son, Frank Junior, gave the reason for his parents' success: they simply read and reread the book of Proverbs and put its principles into practice in their business.

As the Yubetas discovered, truth is absolute. You can build your life on it. Truth does not change. It's always the same, a constant. It's the same for every member of society, rich or poor, leader or ordinary citizen, CEO or floor sweeper. And we can know truth.

This is so important for us to know these days, as postmodernism batters us with the opposite idea—that there are no absolutes. This view came to the West from philosophers of the nineteenth century, but the East has believed the same thing for thousands of years. Most Asian religions teach that truth changes and that you can't know it anyway. The Mahayana Buddhists in Nepal have a saying: if you are asleep, dreaming you are a butterfly, when you're awake how do you know you're not a butterfly asleep, dreaming you're a person?

This kind of thinking has swept the West. In universities, professors of social sciences teach that truth is relative. This philosophy is growing in popularity. Do these statements sound familiar? *That may be true for you, but it's not true for me. There is no such thing as absolute truth. Everything is relative. We all have truth, but it's different truth.*

If this is so, why teach at all? Why should we try to learn? Why have a university?

At the dawn of the twenty-first century the U.S. economy was rocked by scandals in Enron, WorldCom, and other large corporations. Many thousands lost everything they had. Retired people had to go back to work because their pension plans disappeared. What caused the downfall of Enron and WorldCom? It was "creative" accounting practices, making it look like these companies were making more money than they were, inflating the prices of their stock.

The news shocked the public. The news media reacted as if the unbelievable had happened. We should have seen it coming. A recent poll by the Barna Group of Ventura, California, found that Americans no longer believe there is such a thing as moral absolutes. By a three-to-one margin (64 percent to 22 percent), adults said truth is always relative to the person and his or her situation.[9] This kind of thinking will undermine our societies in many ways, including our financial institutions. After all, if you don't believe in unchanging principles of right and wrong, what will keep your accountants and bookkeepers honest?

Science Depends on Absolute Truth

Even though other parts of Western universities are teaching relative truth, professors of physical science still depend upon absolutes. The scientific method says that you can discover truth by recognizing and stating a problem, creating a hypothesis, collecting all available data, conducting experiments, reaching conclusions, and publishing the findings. This method depends on the premise that truth does not change and that we can know it.

The vast technological advances of the Western world would not have been possible without thinking based on the biblical principle of absolute truth. To put it in easy terms, in order to reach the moon, it makes a difference which way you point your rocket—up or down. A suspension bridge stretching across San Francisco Bay can bear the weight of hundreds of thousands of cars, trucks, and trains for years and years because it was built upon absolute truths that do not change and can be known. Think about it. Would you want to get on an airplane if the laws of physics were changing every day?

The Evil Trinity

Relativity of truth does not work in science, and it doesn't work in morals either. It may take longer to see the results in everyday life, but it matters whether we live according to truth or live according to lies. Presently, the standards of living in Western nations are the best in the world because leaders, even those who are not followers of Christ, still work partly on biblical principles. The echo of God's voice still reverberates in our constitutions, laws, languages, and cultures. Besides, in the West believers control more than 50 percent of the wealth.[10] Yet with just a few generations of unchecked greed, corruption, and injustice, Western nations can sink into poverty.

Just look at the many nations held in poverty today by the evil trinity of greed, corruption, and injustice. A few years ago, I visited Congo, then called Zaire. The dictator, Mobutu, was dominating and exploiting Congo. He had accumulated enormous personal wealth through corruption. Mobutu had enough in his personal Swiss bank accounts to pay off the national debts of every African nation and still be the continent's richest man. While I was visiting Congo, the banks collapsed. I tried to change money, but the teller said he couldn't help me—they had no money in the bank. And yet Congo has vast quantities of gold, silver, diamonds, copper, oil, and many other valuable commodities. Despite its great resources, it is one of the poorest countries on earth. It is a tragic history: colonial powers pillaged Congo for years; then greedy dictators and warlords began robbing her.

We Can Lose It All

Now we are seeing this kind of corruption spreading in the West. We've seen recent examples in Western governments, in the United Nations, and in the business world. Representatives from global corporations working in new markets are increasingly pressured to go along with local practices of bribes and kickbacks. They're told it is "the price of doing business" in certain parts of the world.

An international advocacy group called Transparency International has been working to fight corruption in government and business worldwide. The group publishes a *Corruption Perception Index* to bring international attention to this entrenched evil.[11] As believers, we can only applaud this organization's efforts as it seeks to stem the spread of corruption.

However, issuing an index and calling a press conference will never be enough. Without standards of truth, who's to say what is corrupt and what is not? We need to cling to the Bible. Because of it, we can know absolute truth. In the Word of God we can discover truth that makes us free.

Chapter 19

We Are Responsible
to Live According
to the Truth

We also find the fourth nation-changing principle in the early chapters of Genesis: we are responsible to live according to the truth. God gave Adam and Eve responsibility not only to take care of the garden but also to avoid eating from one certain tree. We all know the tragedy that happened when they acted irresponsibly and dismissed the truth, choosing to listen to the lies of the serpent instead.

Today, God continues to give us truth, which we are responsible to obey.[1] Because we can know truth, we have the responsibility to order our lives accordingly and to seek after more truth.[2]

We cannot escape this reality, even if we try to deny the existence of God. A friend of mine, Friedrich Schock, a retired German industrialist, has also been involved in political leadership in his country. He told me of a meeting in Berlin in the days leading up to the collapse of the Soviet Union. In the meeting, Herr Schock heard the Soviet minister of culture and religion say that no nation can be governed unless there is morality among its people. And the Soviet minister said there could be no morality without religion—

he added that he was an atheist, so he didn't understand why this was true!

The Soviet minister was speaking the truth despite himself. Morality has its source in a righteous God who is goodness itself and who always chooses to do good. God created us as moral beings who know right from wrong and are responsible to choose between them. When we choose the good, we choose the truth and are living the way God created us to. This brings blessings to our countries.

The founders of the United States of America knew their new system of government would work only with responsible, moral citizens. One of those founders, Samuel Adams, said, "A general dissolution of principles and manners will more surely overthrow the liberties of America than the whole force of the common enemy. While the people are virtuous, they cannot be subdued; but when once they lose their virtue, they will be ready to surrender their liberties to the first external or internal invader."[3]

Despite what you often hear, Scripture and faith deeply influenced the vast majority of the Founding Fathers.[4] In one review of fifteen thousand writings of the Founding Fathers of America, 94 percent of their quotes were based directly or indirectly on the Bible.[5]

Crumbling Foundations

Have Americans held on to the ideals of their Founding Fathers? Has the country of my birth been living responsibly, using wisely the blessings it has inherited? No, far from it. My heart grieves when I realize how far America has departed from its biblical foundations.

Daniel Webster, a great U.S. senator and secretary of state for three presidents in the nineteenth century, said, "Let us not forget the religious character of our origin. Our fathers were brought hither by their high veneration for the Christian religion.... They sought to incorporate its principles with the elements of their society, and to diffuse its influence through all their institutions, civil, political, or literary."[6]

America has received much truth and is responsible to live by it. Who knows what catastrophes face America if we continue to abandon this great heritage?

Responsibility=Response According to Ability

Responsible choices and behavior are called *righteousness*. Irresponsibility is called *sin*. The Book teaches us throughout its pages that whenever people obey God, they receive certain blessings. When they disobey, they receive curses.

When we hear words such as *blessings* or *curses*, we might imagine God stepping in each time to bring these about. Instead, I believe it is the law of sowing and reaping that is responsible. Certain actions bring certain results, automatically. Even organically.

Think of responsibility as "response according to one's ability to obey the truth." Protesters often call for more rights, for more authority. But have you ever seen a crowd of demonstrators shouting for more responsibility? Usually we want good fruit without good roots.

Picture a nation as a tree. It is rooted in the soil of its worldview—that is, the nation's general view of reality. What a nation believes to be true forms its roots. From those roots grows the trunk—the nation's values. The tree's branches are laws, policies, and practices. The leaves are various forms of cultural expression. The fruit is produced—either freedom and prosperity or bondage and poverty. Finally, the seeds within the fruit begin the process all over again, filling the earth as they are scattered by the sowers.

Can you count the number of seeds in a fruit? Yes. But you cannot count the potential fruit in a seed. The fruit of the tree—the multiplication of blessings or curses—comes from the roots and the trunk—the belief system and values of a country. A belief system held by a critical mass of a nation's population can bring either the benefits of truth or the ruin of lies.

In recent years we have seen more and more countries wanting to become democracies. But for democracy to work, it must have responsible citizens. You cannot enjoy all the fruits of democracy without the roots and trunk of biblical truth and morality. In order for democracy to function best, a country must have a critical number of citizens relying on the Word of God as their manual for government and every part of society.

The *Minority* Rules

In democracies we speak of the rule of the majority. But the Bible doesn't speak of majorities. It speaks of the power of a righteous remnant, or minority.[7] God's Word shows what a determined few can do to change the course of an entire country. One example was Gideon. He and a few good men overthrew a more powerful, wicked majority and brought Israel back to new obedience and faith in God.[8]

The same has been true throughout history: often, the minority rules. We saw in chapter 14 how a minority of believers in Geneva read about God's mercy and how the Old Testament cities of refuge gave them the idea of helping "refugees."[9] A righteous minority put that biblical principle into practice in Geneva, building extra stories onto their houses to take in refugees. They created a legacy of mercy toward refugees that lingers in Switzerland until today.

It's important to keep this in mind, or we will feel defeated before we start. Maybe you have thought to yourself, *I'm trying hard to do the right thing, but I'm just one person. So many are living such ungodly lives! How can my life make a difference?*

Remember, Jesus told us we are the salt of the earth.[10] Think about that for a minute. Salt is a humble substance, *an extraordinarily ordinary* element. When you add it to a dish, it is invisible. But a very, very small amount makes all the difference—adding flavor and also keeping food from spoiling.

We don't have to be big and powerful. We don't have to be the person on TV every night or the world's greatest expert in our field. All we have to do is maintain our saltiness. Be who God made us to be and do our part. If we don't do this, if we lose our saltiness, as it talks about in Matthew 5, we will be worthless, of no use in the building of God's kingdom.

Remember who is in charge of the whole project: the mighty Creator of the universe. He's the one who has the complete picture in mind, who knows just what needs to be done and what the end should be. He's the one who designed you, and he's the one who has the power to accomplish his plan. And he's the one who will use you and your obedience in just the right way to help bring healing to a broken world.

Chapter 20

Why Nations
Are Rich or Poor

What tears down a nation? Simply abandoning the Word of God—especially the foundational ideas found in the first chapters of Genesis. When a nation casts these aside, it begins to self-destruct. There are no exceptions. No leadership or power or economic status is permanent.

Look again at the foundational truths from the Word of God... but this time, paired with what happens if we abandon the Word of God:

- Who God is: we exchange the truth about who God is for a lie.
- Who we are: we weaken our understanding of who we are, created in his image, male and female, equal in value.
- Unchanging, knowable truth: we lose the idea that truth is real and unchanging and that we can know it.
- The responsibility of man to live according to the truth: we deny we are responsible for our actions, both individually and corporately.

If a nation loses these foundations, it can be reduced to an undeveloped country. And it can happen within three or four generations.

What Makes the Difference?

Come with me to a scene I have often observed. We could see this outside any Western embassy in any developing nation. A tropical sun blisters the heads and shoulders of people standing in a long line. They are wearing their best clothes, almost as if they are going to a wedding or to church.

Occasionally, the door opens a crack and a whiff of air conditioning escapes as they allow one more person in. The rest remain standing outside, shifting their weight, wiping away sweat. Mothers try to hush fretful children. Most have been waiting since before sunup. As noon approaches, the line grows, snaking around the outside walls. But no one gives up. People wait patiently for their turn to apply for a visa, hoping to move to a better country. Those who don't get inside today will come again tomorrow, and the next day, and the next. No inconvenience is too great.

People who want a better future for themselves and their children stand in lines at the embassies of all Western nations. But no one stands in a long line outside the embassy of Cuba or Sudan or India. Why not? Why aren't millions of people trying to become permanent residents of those nations? What makes the difference between nations? Why are some very wealthy and others very poor, causing their people to leave in hopes of a better life?

Shackling Human Potential

In more than fifty years of continual travel among the nations, I have observed three things that cause a country to become poor, its people unable to fulfill their human potential. These three things, which we called the evil trinity in chapter 18, are unbridled greed, corruption, and injustice. All three are opposite to God's character, to the way he designed us to live, and to our responsibility to live according to the truth.

I've seen the effects of these three evils in one poor country after another. This is not to say that everyone in those nations is greedy, corrupt, and unjust. But these characteristics prevail. If a critical mass of people in powerful positions have unbridled greed, corruption comes out of that greed—giving and taking bribes, and extortion. Great injustices inevitably follow.

What do I mean by "critical mass"? It isn't a certain percentage point, but perhaps we could say 25 percent to 35 percent. It isn't even a majority. You'll know critical mass has been reached when you see the cultural tone of a society begin to change. It's a tipping point.

Some years ago as I rode in a taxi, my Filipino driver complained about how corrupt President Marcos was. I asked, "How do you know he's corrupt?"

"He even paid people to vote for him," the man answered.

"How do you know that?" I asked.

"Well, he paid me, and I voted for him."

The taxi driver didn't see that Marcos wasn't the only one who was corrupt. Dishonest government officials can operate only if they find dishonest people to cooperate with them.

Every country has those who have given themselves over to greed, corruption, and injustice. But when such people become the dominant influence, they tear down their country.

In the same way, not everyone has to follow God for a nation to begin to rise. We have been looking at the ways nations destroy themselves. But the same principles work in the opposite direction. Any nation that keeps greed in check with the spirit of generosity, any country that develops righteousness and justice in government, can grow its economy and its freedoms.

"Why Are We So Poor?"

"Why are we so poor?" I was asked that question in a meeting with the cabinet and top leaders of a West African nation. In September of 1996, I received a telephone call asking if I could come and meet with President Mathieu Kérékou of Benin.

President Kérékou was a former dictator of Benin. In the past he was a communist and an atheist. He was a close friend of Kim Il Sung of North Korea. He even went to North Korea, the strictest communist nation in the world, seeking to pattern his country after it.

In 1990, President Kérékou saw that communism was crumbling around the world. He decided democracy was better than communism, so he announced to the people, "You can choose your next leader." He scheduled a free election, and his people voted him out of office.

Four years later, Mathieu Kérékou found Christ and brought his usual enthusiasm to his new faith. Where before he had been a radical atheist and a communist, now he became an eager follower of Jesus. Immediately he began to witness, sharing the Lord with the people of his land. In 1996, they voted him in as president.

President Kérékou had been reading my books. I guess he felt he could trust me. So now he invited me to come teach him how to be a leader according to the Word of God. Most people in his nation are either Muslim or practitioners of voodoo, but he believed that could change.

After I met with him privately, President Kérékou asked me to speak to his cabinet, the ministers and their deputies, about thirty in all. After I addressed the group, the leaders of Benin had questions. One of the cabinet members asked, "Why are we so poor? We're one of the fifteen poorest nations on earth." Then he tried to answer his own question: "Benin has only five natural resources." And he named them.

I said, "You're not poor because you lack natural resources. Look at Switzerland! They have very few resources, and yet they're rich." I went on to say that Switzerland's prosperity came because people want their products. Whether they make a chocolate bar or a watch, everyone knows the Swiss will make it with precision. Furthermore, you can't have precision without integrity. The Swiss have integrity. They also have a high regard for justice and generosity—every village has some kind of charitable project, especially for refugees.

"You need a critical mass of people who have integrity, who have character," I told President Kérékou and his cabinet. "Benin will have prosperity when it has enough people with this kind of character."

I looked around the room. I could see that people were really listening. When I left, I felt like I had given them the truth—something that could change their country. Real change will come for Benin as it will for other countries—when they turn away from such things as voodoo and as more and more individuals are transformed by submitting to the Word of God. It takes more than a generation. No nation is built overnight. Building character takes time, in individuals and in nations.

Integrity is so important for a country's economy. We don't trust people who cheat to get the critical jobs, like engineering or constructing skyscrapers or manufacturing airplanes. Integrity is also key when handling investments, banking, and transactions of all kinds. If a person cheats, he or she will cheat on big things as well as little ones. You don't want dishonest people building your bridges, because the bridges won't stand. Neither do you want dishonest people handling your retirement funds.

The Haves and the Have-Nots

It's not enough for a nation to have a few honest people. A nation must have a critical mass. There has to be a certain percentage of people in a population who are honest and precise if that nation is to have a good economy. Think of the nations where good engineering jobs are done. Consider the places where people are investing their savings. Look at countries where automobiles or other products of precision are made. These nations will always have a healthy percentage of citizens with strong integrity.

People, not physical things, are a nation's true resources, Consider this: how much is a handful of sand worth? Two pennies? One cent? Not even that. Yet it's possible to turn a handful of sand into microchips. Somebody became a billionaire and created jobs for millions of people by acting on that idea.

People using their God-given gifts within a free society produce wealth. It's not a matter of resources. Some of the poorest countries on earth have incredible natural riches: countries such as Sierra Leone, Congo, and Mozambique. Some very wealthy nations, such as Switzerland, Singapore, and Japan have few resources. What makes the difference? Why have some countries become rich while others remain poor?

God Bless America...and Every Other Nation on Earth!

Has God blessed some nations more than others? No, I believe God is impartial and just. The most-quoted verse of the Bible,

John 3:16, tells us that God so loved *the world*. God has given gifts to all people. How we use his gifts determines our success—as individuals and as nations.

God's greatest gift was his Son, Jesus, whom he gave to save us from our sins. He has given us another gift, relevant to all peoples— the Bible. How can you describe a book that has foundational understanding for every human problem, steps to health and happiness, and building blocks for greatness in every part of society? That book is priceless. It is a real national treasure.

The Book is the greatest blessing an individual can have, next to receiving redemption through Jesus Christ. This Book is not just instructions on how to get to heaven, though that is wonderful and essential. It also gives principles for individuals and nations to answer every problem on earth. Having the Bible and applying its truth in each area of society is what makes a country rich and free.

You might already be thinking of exceptions to this. What about Japan? If applying the Bible is the reason a country becomes prosperous, why is Japan—a nation with few believers—so well off? We will discuss Japan and other special cases in part 4.

Notice that it is not just possessing the Bible but studying it and applying it that bring blessing. Every treasure needs to be used. Jesus showed in the Parable of the Talents that he expects us to invest our treasure, not hoard it unused.[1]

Perhaps you've heard of a person who seemed to be poor, eating a meager diet, living in a ramshackle house, and going about in ragged clothes. After his death, to everyone's surprise, they found the old miser had a stash of cash hidden under his mattress, never used. We can be doing that with the Bible. It's a treasure that we need to get out and into circulation. We need to put it to work, investing it in our lives and in those around us. It's only by tapping into the Bible that we can realize its power to transform us and our nations.

Part 4

Are There Exceptions to the Rule?

Chapter 21

Japan:
Partial Obedience,
Partial Blessing

Throughout this book we have considered one basic idea: whenever a critical mass of people apply the truths found in God's Book, their lives and their nations are transformed.

Now let's look at seeming contradictions of this idea. What about strides made by the Egyptians, the Chinese, the Arabs, and other great cultures of the past? People who did not have The Book built the pyramids, used embalming techniques that we still cannot duplicate, invented gunpowder and paper, discovered the concept of zero in mathematics, and achieved other remarkable things throughout history.

Knowledge is always ready to be discovered whenever people apply their God-given talents to search it out. What we're talking about is the *degree* to which knowledge and wealth become widespread. While these cultures without The Book were able to discover truths God had written into creation—such as mathematical formulas and methods to build the pyramids—knowledge did not transform their societies. Most people remained poor and ignorant. The explosion of wealth and knowledge came only after the Bible was put into more people's hands.

What about Japan?

What about a modern-day success story like Japan—a nation where only 6 percent follow Christ?[1] Japan is wealthy and productive, yet her culture is not based on the Bible. How can this be? Does this exception disprove our thinking? Japan has one of the strongest economies in the world. It dominates the electronics industry and makes reliable watches like Seiko and prized automobiles such as Toyota and Honda. The bridge out of Kobe is a triumph of engineering, one of the most intricate, precisely built bridges in all the world.

Why have the Japanese excelled? Because their culture upholds a biblical truth—honesty with regard to material possessions and business dealings. Some of that honesty came from old cultural practices. Other influences were from godly people behind the scenes, working at critical times in Japan's history.

I stood in the main train station in Osaka in the early 1970s, in an enormous underground area filled with shops. I was there with Jonathan, a missionary's son who had grown up in Japan. Crowds of Japanese rushed past us, some of the one million people who pass through that station every day.

I looked down. To my surprise, my young friend had left his wallet lying on top of his suitcase on the floor. He wasn't paying any attention, so I kept a careful eye on his wallet myself, in case anyone snatched it.

"Loren, come over here. I want to show you something," Jonathan said, walking away toward one of the shops.

I protested. "Jonathan! What about your money and your suitcase?"

"Aw, it's okay," he said. "This is Japan."

Despite my misgivings, we left his suitcase with his wallet on top and walked over to a shop. The huge crowds of people prevented us from seeing his suitcase from there. After about ten minutes we returned. His things were untouched.

Later I told a missionary in Tokyo about the experience. He said, "You could have left a stack of money on that suitcase all day and it wouldn't have been taken. Unless a foreigner came by."

Of course, Japan has changed in recent years because of drug usage and other problems. But many are still very honest about personal possessions.

Partial Obedience, Partial Blessing

When I told this story to some Japanese pastors, one of them said, "Wait a minute! We're not that honest. We lie to each other all the time. We do this so that we won't lose face."

"Yes," I said, "and though you are number two in your economy worldwide, you have a high rate of suicide, alcoholism, and dysfunctional families. You are blessed in your economy but not in your relationships."[2]

The Japanese pastor revealed an important fact. When you partially obey God's Book, you have partial blessing. The Japanese have been blessed economically because of their honesty regarding things. But they have been plagued by social problems because of their dishonesty in personal matters.

Hidden Yeast in Japan

There is another factor in Japan's economic success—the little-known influence of one particular person who made a tremendous impact on the country.

Jesus used yeast as a metaphor for his kingdom, a kingdom that exists inside people but affects all of society.[3] When I was a small boy, I used to watch my mother make homemade rolls. She showed me the little block of yeast and explained how little it takes, hidden within the dough, to change the whole mixture.

Who can say at what precise point the yeast permeates the whole, changing it? No wonder Jesus used this to explain the kingdom of God, showing how a few people can quietly but powerfully affect a nation.

William Merrell Vories

This is an apt comparison to what happened to Japan in the twentieth century. A man hidden from the rest of the world was one of the most important leavening agents in the country. I learned of him rather recently, even though I have gone to Japan many times.

A few years ago in Switzerland, my wife, Darlene, and I were staying in the home of some friends while they were away. As I stood in front of their packed bookcase, my eyes were drawn to an old book called *Adventurers for God*. *That sounds interesting,* I thought, and I pulled it off the shelf. It fell open to the chapter on Japan, to the story of William Merrell Vories. I settled in to read this book, written by Clarence Hall, senior editor of *Reader's Digest*, in the days following World War II.[4]

Hall told how Vories arrived in Japan in 1905. Although he was trained as an architect, Vories went to Japan determined to win people to Christ. He wasn't a missionary in the classic sense, but he decided he would live the life of Jesus before the Japanese. Vories went to one of the most remote parts of Japan's interior because he wanted to "find some spot too inconspicuous to appeal to any other missionary."[5]

Vories got a job teaching English in Omi-Hachiman (now called Shiga Prefecture). In his off-hours he held Bible studies. As he made converts among the young men, their families kicked them out. Soon many were living with the missionary in his small home. Before long Vories needed more space, so he raised the money to build a larger facility, with dormitories and room for Bible study and recreation.

Trouble soon found Vories in the hinterland. He won so many young people to Christ that he alarmed the Buddhist priests. The priests stirred up ruffians to attack the new believers with baseball bats and got the provincial newspaper to write a series of articles denouncing Vories and Christianity. Ultimately they pressured the school to fire Vories from his teaching post.

After just two years on the job, Vories found himself in a distant land with no means of support and a community of young men looking to him for guidance.

A Radical Experiment

While struggling in prayer one night, asking God what to do, Vories thought about his architectural training. What if he were to start a company? Founding an architectural firm in such a remote place went against all commercial wisdom. But he did it, immediately setting out to teach the trade to his young converts.

Within a short time, Vories and his band of architectural brothers were running the most influential design firm in Japan.

Vories discovered how to construct buildings that could withstand Japan's frequent earthquakes. By the 1950s, the firm had designed and built 2,800 structures, located all over the country. However, it was the radical way they demonstrated Christ in their personal lives and professional work that really made a mark on the country.

The men formed a "business with a mission," eventually called the Omi Brotherhood. Even though they were making substantial money as architects, they took only enough for bare living expenses. Vories and the others in the brotherhood each lived on an average of sixty-two dollars a month, no matter what his role was.[6]

The men poured the rest back into a wide range of evangelistic and humanitarian endeavors—establishing churches, other preaching points, and Sunday schools. The Omi brothers paid for seminary training for scores of pastors, then supported them as they ministered. The brotherhood also founded a tuberculosis sanatorium and many schools. On weekends and in the evenings, they left their drawing tables to preach and teach in the villages. Their Sunday schools and Bible classes grew into more churches. The brotherhood also mailed postcards containing the gospel message to virtually every address in Japan.

Mentholatum, the "Jesus Medicine"

Over time the Omi Brotherhood diversified, starting educational, industrial, religious, and philanthropic departments. Vories was also able to get manufacturing rights for Mentholatum ointment in Japan. After designing a model factory, he hired hundreds of workers. Soon they were distributing eight million packages of Mentholatum across Japan each year. The Omi brothers printed a special label for every jar, inviting people to learn more about Christ in a Bible correspondence course. This led to thousands of new believers all over Japan. In fact, in rural Japan people started calling Mentholatum the "Jesus medicine."

Through all the brotherhood's undertakings, Vories sought for "a practical demonstration of *Christianized* economics in the world today."[7]

Closing Down for Repentance

Perhaps the brotherhood's greatest contribution was teaching Japan a new way to run a corporation. Until then, corruption and graft were considered normal—the way to do business. Vories made it clear that "Christian principles will be applied to every job from drawing board to completed structure."[8] That ruled out giving or taking bribes. Offering the brotherhood a bribe meant losing them as your architects—or for contractors, forfeiting the chance to work on the buildings.

The Omi brothers also established humane working conditions for workers. They set up a forty-eight-hour workweek and didn't allow any work on the Sabbath. They upheld the value of taking good care of employees, ruled out excessive salaries for top workers, and concentrated on serving the country by producing necessary commodities of good quality at reasonable prices. As a result, no one ever staged a strike or a walkout in any of their plants.

No wonder industrialists came from all over Japan to marvel at Vories's modern factories and to study his management principles. When these industrialists asked him to lecture on his successes, Vories took the opportunity to teach biblical principles of economics, leadership, and business.

The brotherhood enforced personal integrity within their ranks as well. When four young members were caught in a moral lapse in 1918, Vories made public contrition by shutting down their offices and suspending all work throughout their company for three days. He said, "Only an organization that stands ready to kill itself for the sake of its principles is qualified to live."[9]

Vories married a nobleman's daughter in 1919. Some feared this dainty aristocrat named Maki would compromise his life of discipline and devotion. Instead she moved into a humble cottage with him and threw her energies into developing a modern system of schools, playgrounds, nursery schools, night schools, and continuing educational programs for their workers.

In 1940 a prominent Tokyo newspaper hailed Vories as "not only first citizen of Omi-Hachiman, but among the first in all Japan."[10] Vories finally became a Japanese citizen in January of 1941. Eleven months later, the Japanese attack on Pearl Harbor plunged him into his greatest despair.

Chapter 22

Japan's Extreme Makeover

During the war the Omi Brotherhood's industries were slowed, their schools taken over, and their religious work hampered. Younger members were drafted into the army and many were killed. The military leaders seized most of their facilities. Only the Japanese army's need for Mentholatum kept the brotherhood from folding up entirely.

Then military leaders spread the rumor that Vories was an American spy. Emperor Hirohito sent his brother to Omi-Hachiman to show his support, deflecting this attack on the architect/missionary.

During the last seven months of the war, Vories and his wife took refuge in the mountains. They had to forage in the hills for edible leaves and weeds to keep from starving. However, their low estate was reversed quickly when the Allies defeated Japan and the U.S. occupation began. Vories found himself in a unique position— he was born an American but was now a businessman completely versed in Japanese ways, highly thought of throughout the country. He became a liaison between the new government and the American occupational authority, spending time in both the Imperial Palace and the Allied headquarters.

Helping a Former Enemy

During the reconstruction period, Vories again spread the yeast of the gospel and biblical principles. General Douglas MacArthur, Supreme Commander for Allied Powers, set out to remake the former enemy country, instituting a wide range of benevolent reforms. MacArthur famously called for ten thousand missionaries to come and train the Japanese to live in a new way—but only a few hundred answered the call.[1]

Other allies pressured General MacArthur to punish the Japanese people and all their leaders. The Russians threatened to come in and occupy their share of the country to be sure justice was carried out. But MacArthur prevailed. The general wrote to U.S. Secretary of the Treasury Henry Morgenthau saying he wanted "to carry to the land of our vanquished foe the solace and hope and faith of Christian morals."[2]

General MacArthur set ambitious goals for reforming the nation. He lifted all restrictions on political, civil, and religious activities. He brought the worst of Japan's war criminals to justice. He released political prisoners. He launched feeding programs to aid the peasants who had been forced to fight and pay exorbitant taxes during the war. He ordered U.S. troops not to eat any food needed by the people and pleaded with the U.S. government to send more food.

Future Tycoons in Class Photo

In the face of these good-faith efforts, the Japanese people began to believe the United States would help their country.[3] General MacArthur patterned Japan's new constitution after that of the United States. Women got the right to vote, and the first democratically elected assembly made women equal before the law. Soon universities for women opened, and women were elected to office. MacArthur set up the new educational system. He also brought in carefully chosen American businessmen to help the Japanese lay the foundations for a new economy. Years later, I saw a photo in *Forbes* magazine taken during this time. Young Japanese were posing with their American teacher. I read the students' names and recognized several who are now attached to famous brands in the global economy.

The Japanese spent the post–World War II years in a critical time of self-examination. They had fought the war for religious reasons as well as for nationalism. The Japanese believed that their emperor was a god and that their race was superior to every other. When their crushing defeat discredited those beliefs, they were open to new ideas.

Someone who eased the way for them was a man who had earned their trust over the decades—Vories. In *Adventurers for God*, Clarence Hall says, "Under MacArthur's benevolent reforms, strongly underscored with religious faith, Vories found the Japanese clamoring to learn more about Christianity."[4]

The people called on Vories to lecture in universities, hold evangelistic meetings, and meet with government officials to discuss the "spiritual aspects of democracy." The Imperial Palace even summoned him several times to discuss "Christian democracy" with the emperor.[5]

There was one other important change. The new constitution provided for equality among Japan's people. Through Vories's efforts, this new equality included the *Eta*, or "unclean" class who had been segregated for centuries, much like the "untouchables" in India. It was just one more way God brought blessing after the evil of the war years. He forged a new beginning for Japan using a missionary, a general, and a searching people.

When Americans helped the Japanese rebuild their country, including their new constitution, they passed on aspects of U.S. culture that were based on The Book. However, the Japanese honesty regarding material possessions, a basic principle in their culture, went beyond what Americans could teach them. This cultural value, plus the effect of hidden yeast like William Vories and the Omi brothers, has helped bring about the economic resurgence of Japan.

All are responsible to obey God's truth, every person and every nation. In the Old Testament, Deuteronomy 28 says that if we obey the principles of The Book, we will be blessed; if we don't, we will be cursed. If we do what God has said, we will be blessed here on earth, even if we don't have a Bible or know Jesus, the greatest blessing of all. God's principles are relevant, even when followed by unbelievers, as in Japan. On the other hand, if we do not obey principles from God's Word, we will know failure and defeat. This is true for every nation on earth, no matter how great its heritage.

Chapter 23

Africa:
Great Challenges,
Great Hope

I have ministered in every country of Africa, visiting the continent year after year since 1961. I love being in vast congregations of African believers, joining in their exuberant worship and celebration. In December of 2002, I had the privilege of standing in an open parade ground and speaking to more than a million Nigerians at one time. My friend Reinhard Bonnke often preaches to audiences of two million in Africa, seeing large numbers converted and dramatic miracles of healing.

I marvel at Africans' energetic evangelism and church growth. In 1900, less than 10 percent of Africans were followers of Christ. By 2000, that swelled to more than 45 percent who considered themselves part of the church.[1] The number rises to nearly 70 percent for parts of Africa below the Sahara.[2]

African believers are also spreading beyond their own national and regional borders. Many Africans have gone to Europe as missionaries, seeking to revive the flagging faith there. As of 2000, an estimated thirteen thousand African missionaries were serving in cross-cultural settings.[3]

Despite all this, Africa breaks my heart.

Stalked by Tragedy

Across the continent, the people of Africa suffer great personal and economic hardship. Many countries struggle with extreme poverty, famine, drought, corruption, civil war, and disease.[4]

AIDS has cut down a generation, in turn fueling more famine and poverty. In some countries the HIV infection rate reaches 40 percent—more than seven times higher than the world average.[5] With only 10 percent of the world's population, sub-Saharan Africa has nearly two-thirds of all people living with HIV.[6] Almost twenty-six million Africans have AIDS.

We can drown in numbers like these—they are too much to take in. Relief agencies tell of finding entire villages populated only with children, where young girls and boys till the soil, raising food for their younger sisters and brothers. Twelve million African children have lost one or both parents to AIDS.[7] Twelve million! Think of a city one and a half times the size of New York, populated only with orphans.

We struggle to comprehend this, but there's more. Countrymen have slaughtered six million of their neighbors in civil wars in Sierra Leone, Angola, Liberia, Congo, and Sudan.[8] Rwandans killed one million of their own citizens during one hundred grisly days in 1994.[9]

Yet civil wars and the AIDS pandemic are only two of the calamities threatening Africa. There are many more. We grieve and God grieves.

Tribalism, Animism, and Colonialism

Where has the church failed? How can we account for these tragedies in a continent with so many believers? First, we have to question how many of the reported millions of believers are truly loyal to Christ. Animism, particularly worshiping ancestors and clinging to fetishes, continues to cripple many churchgoers.[10] These pagan ways are held firmly in place by an even greater African loyalty—loyalty to the tribes. Tribalism is also at the heart of the civil wars that have killed so many.

There is nothing intrinsically wrong with tribes. Acts 17:26 says God made every nation. The word for "nation" here is *ethné*, which is more like our word for tribes. In Scripture, God blessed tribes whenever they lined up with his Word and threw off the influence of animistic or other nature-based religions around them.[11] Today, the tribes of Africa must break away from centuries of bondage to false beliefs. Wherever loyalty to tribal traditions conflicts with the truth of God's Word, God's way must prevail. That will set Africa free.

We Share the Blame

I believe some of the blame for Africa's plight lies with the church of the West. We have been more faithful at carrying out Jesus' command in Mark 16:15, to *preach the good news of salvation to every person*, than we have been at obeying his command in Matthew 28:19–20, to *teach all nations*. Generations of faithful missionaries have led Africans to Christ. But have we taught them principles from the Word of God on how to raise their families, run their businesses, and govern their countries?

Colonialism also polluted mission work in Africa for more than a hundred years. The same nations who sent missionaries also sent exploiting colonial rulers. The West laid the groundwork years ago for the heartbreaking civil wars we're seeing now. European colonial powers carved up some people groups and lumped others together, drawing national boundaries to suit European interests. Sometimes foreigners with limited understanding of local dynamics placed minority tribes in premium positions over larger tribes.

Perhaps the greatest injury we inflicted was our paternalism toward Africans. For too long, missionaries relegated converts to a kind of perpetual childhood, not training them for leadership. In East Africa, a young man told me, "The missionaries taught us how to read, but the communists gave us something to read." I remember a story I heard in 1961, when colonial rule was ending everywhere. A group of people sat beside the river in Congo, patiently waiting for "freedom" to arrive. They thought it was a thing, something that would arrive in one of the boats on the river.

Where would Africa be today if there had been an African John Calvin or Hans Nielsen Hauge in the nineteenth century, searching the Scriptures, teaching people how to build a godly country?

One Bible, One Race

The paternalism of the past runs long and deep and wide. After I stood and preached at a meeting in Nigeria in 1961, telling the Nigerian youth they should go out as missionaries, a veteran missionary scolded me. "Don't you know God doesn't intend for Africans to be missionaries? *We* are missionaries. *They* are natives."

I was surprised by his reaction and told him, "Their Bibles say the same thing as mine."

That racism still exists today. Here's the other side of the coin. Recently, I was watching a panel on TV. Leading U.S. clergy were discussing a sexual scandal that had drawn a lot of media attention. One on the panel, an evangelical pastor, implied that our ideas about sexual immorality are culturally based, suggesting that standards of immorality are different for African-Americans than they are for whites. That would mean that the Ten Commandments don't apply to black people the way they do to white people.

These two examples—from Nigeria and the United States—actually reflect racism. My answer is to say there is only one race—the human race. We are all descended from Adam and Eve. And we have one Bible for this one race of people. The truths of The Book apply to everyone. We are all created in God's image. We can all know truth. And we are all responsible to live according to truth in every area.

Character develops one decision at a time. Personal salvation can come instantly, but character must be cultivated over time. We must teach the principles of God's Word to every nation and every people. As Hans Nielsen Hauge told his followers, "This is God's Book, and it's for every area of life." Hauge believed it and applied it. Norway's history stands as a monument to how quickly The Book can change a nation.

I have great hope for Africa. I believe we can see it healed and turned around. I see several signs of encouragement.

African Heroes

Over the past few years I have noticed something—Africans both on the continent and in diaspora are rising to prominence. For instance...

Until 2007, the Secretary-General for the United Nations was an African—Kofi Annan. One of the most powerful people in the world has been U.S. Secretary of State, Condoleezza Rice, an African-American. Her predecessor, Colin Powell is also African-American. The highest paid person in entertainment is another black—billionaire and philanthropist Oprah Winfrey, who heads up a multimillion-dollar enterprise of publishing and broadcast media. And what would the world of sports be without Africans, and Africans in diaspora? Basketball, baseball, soccer, football, track and field, tennis, boxing—blacks dominate Olympic sports and professional sports of all kinds. From Pele to Michael Jordan to Tiger Woods to the Williams sisters, many of the finest athletes are descendants of Africans.

African descendants have succeeded in entertainment, on TV and in movie roles. Talented comedians like Bill Cosby and many, many more have brought laughter to millions. Halle Berry, Denzel Washington, Jamie Foxx, and Morgan Freeman are just some who've won Oscars for great dramatic performances.

Sons and daughters of Africa have enriched the arts, creating new forms of music in jazz, gospel, blues, rock, reggae, hip-hop, and rap. The melodies and rhythms of these music forms have spread across America and around the world. In all of them I can hear the distinctive beat I went to sleep with many a night in Africa.

These are just a few examples, but I believe there is a trend here. God is showing us he has great things in store for Africans—those at home and those in diaspora. As I have traveled to every country of Africa, I've caught a glimpse of God's dreams for these people. He has lavished such beauty and treasures on that continent.

What Are God's Plans for Africa?

Come with me to Africa. The greatest desert in the world, the Sahara, takes your breath away with its rolling dunes, golden in the sun. Going to a zoo will seem tame after you've visited the Kalahari or after you've seen the clouds of dust and heard the thunder of thousands of zebras galloping across the Serengeti. Come, stand on a mountain in Kenya and look at a distant blue lake with a belt of soft pink—the color is from multitudes of flamingos wading around its edges. Go down on the plain and watch the elephants and giraffes amble by, stopping to nibble off the tops of trees. Your skin prickles at the roar of mating lions or the ripple of crocodiles sliding by in the water.

If you visit the vast emerald jungles in the west or the massive Rift Valley in the east, you will think you're in the Garden of Eden.

Stand on the plains and look up at the towering peak of Kilimanjaro. Your eyes scan the horizon, taking in towering rocks and two-story anthills. Sparkling lakes are big enough to have populated islands. If you have time, you can go see great rivers like the Nile, flowing north from Lake Victoria in Uganda all the way through Egypt to spill into the Mediterranean. The Congo River cascades west to the Atlantic. The 1,600-mile-long Zambezi flows east, pounding over one of the most beautiful waterfalls in the world, Victoria Falls, finally emptying into the Indian Ocean in Mozambique.

The World's Greatest Riches

Our great artist God has displayed these and other wonders in Africa. What are his plans for this continent and this people? He hid more gold here, more diamonds, plutonium, and copper than in any other place on earth. Africa has enough arable land to feed a large portion of the earth. The continent has more hydroelectric potential than all the rest of the world put together, as well as an abundance of coal and oil.[12]

Wisely used by and for Africans, the continent's resources could contribute significantly to new health and prosperity. Unfortunately, for too long Africa's people have been enslaved, raped, abused, dismissed by prejudice, hated, or just ignored. Their rich resources have often been collected and used by others—even stolen—with little if any benefit going to the Africans. Instead, their value has attracted foreign exploitation, enriching dictators and warlords, bringing bloodshed, starvation, and even modern forms of black-on-black slavery.

But God has not forgotten them. During the twentieth century, the number of believers in Africa grew from 8 million to 351 million.[13] Now African congregations are sending out missionaries and spiritual leaders to every continent. A Nigerian, Pastor Sunday

Adelaja, leads the largest church in Europe. I preached in his church in Kyiv (Kiev), Ukraine, with thousands of members at its base and branches throughout the nations.

In Nigeria, Dr. E. A. Adeboye has gathered the most believers at one location in the history of the church—an estimated seven million people for a prayer meeting from 6:00 PM to 6:00 AM for three nights in 1998.[14] Pastor Adeboye told me his church has pioneered thousands of churches in fifty-nine nations.

An African-American, Dr. T. D. Jakes, pastors one of the largest churches in America, The Potter's House in Dallas, with 35,000 members.[15]

Recently, I visited the cramped holding room in Zanzibar where Arab traders once sold multiplied thousands of African slaves to other Arabs, Europeans, and Americans. I saw the auction block under a tree where they stood—humiliated, beaten, and sold like animals. I could only wonder at the swift rise to greatness that Africans have achieved.

I have so much hope for Africa. One who gives me hope is George Kinoti, a zoology professor at Nairobi University. Mr. Kinoti is like an African Hauge or Carey. He is working to transform his nation of Kenya.[16] As he and others like him rise up in African countries, discipling the millions who are coming to Jesus, who knows what we will see happen? I believe Africa can be the continent of great light, an example to the whole world of the redeeming power of God and his Word. When a critical number of Africans don't just read the Bible or quote it but apply it in their lives, Africa will change. It will change radically.

Chapter 24

Latin America:
Hope Delayed

I've loved Latin America for a very long time. Some of my earliest childhood memories are of sunbaked towns along the Mexican border in Arizona and California where I made my first friends with Mexican people. As a teenager in Los Angeles, I liked listening to Hispanic radio stations, practicing a new language. My first mission trip, at age seventeen, was to Mexico. And as an adult, I have visited every nation of Latin America.

How do we view Latin America in terms of The Book? At first glance, it's a region that seems to have been overwhelmingly Christian for centuries. And God has richly endowed this part of the world with every kind of natural resource. But for much of its history, corrupt, unstable governments have plagued Latin America. Great divisions split people apart with a handful of wealthy on top, masses of poor on the bottom, and hardly any middle class in between. How could Latin American nations have the church for so long and yet not have the blessings we've described?

Two major factors have weakened the effect of the Bible in Latin America: the spirit of the Middle East and the problem of syncretism—a mixing of Christianity and paganism.

The Spirit of the Middle East in Latin America

First, the spirit and worldview of the Middle East have permeated Latin culture. Remember that the Moors, a Muslim people, ruled most of the Iberian Peninsula, which would later become Spain and Portugal, for hundreds of years. They came "evangelizing" by the sword in the eighth century. The Moors weren't expelled until the end of the fifteenth century when Queen Isabella and King Ferdinand conquered the remainder of Spain in 1492. When the Spanish first landed in the New World, Spain's Christian-dominated government was still quite new.

Several signs show the influence of the Middle East on Spain and Portugal. You can see it in the Spanish language. For instance, the Spanish and the Arabic words for "shirt" are *camisa* and *kamis*. The two languages also use virtually the same word for "pants," *pantalones* and *bantalon*. The characteristic Spanish exclamation, ¡*Ojalá!* comes from *inshallah*, or "whatever Allah wills."

When you look at word connections, you can see the links between ideas and worldviews. In this way you can discern that Spain and Portugal took on the spirit of the Middle East. They share the same fatalism. The belief of "whatever Allah wills" corresponds with the Spanish *que será será*—"whatever will be, will be." These phrases reveal a common belief that our choices don't matter—the future is predetermined.

Another similarity involves the *machismo* idea of masculinity in Latin culture, which corresponds to a similar concept in the Middle East. For instance, a critical mass of both cultures expect men to dominate women. Women do not have value in themselves. They only have value because of what they contribute to men. And both cultures have a double standard when it comes to acceptable behavior for each gender. By religious law a Muslim man can have four wives. In Latin custom it has been acceptable for a man to have multiple mistresses as well as a wife.

Crueler Than Their Masters

Still another similarity lies in the history of conversion by the sword. Muslims have been known to spread their religion by the harshest of means. They used their swords to convert the people of the Iberian Peninsula. Some historians say the Muslims learned conversion by the sword from Christians, going back to Constantine. But for whatever reason, this brutality was absorbed and passed on, bringing much bloodshed in the name of God. As the peoples of Iberia overthrew the Moors, they went out themselves, conquering new lands and repeating the same behavior. In fact, they were even more oppressive and less tolerant than the Moors had been in Iberia.

Queen Isabella required that when *conquistadores* went with swords in their hands, they would have missionaries by their sides.[1] Their excuse for conquest was that they were bringing the gospel to the pagans. But the conquerors raped the women and stole the gold. One account tells of Balboa's men cutting up Indians like "butchers cutting up beef and mutton for market."[2] Spaniards commonly used dogs to fight these "naked people," to tear them to pieces.[3]

Imagine what it was like to hear the gospel in such a setting. Under Spanish law Catholics could not be enslaved. The natives were thus given a choice. One would be asked through an interpreter, "Do you want to be a Christian?"

"No."

"Take him away—he can be a slave in the silver mines."

Then they asked the next person, "Do you want to be a Christian?"

"Oh, yes! I've always wanted to be a Christian."

Then they'd have the "convert" kneel down and turn him over to the missionary to be baptized.

This was how many indigenous peoples were "evangelized." In his article "How Did Native Americans Respond to Christianity?" Thomas S. Giles tells of a Spanish official in Central America in 1514, going from village to village. "Before they entered, they declared loudly: 'Princes and Indians, there is one God, one pope, and one king of Castile who is lord of this country. Come at once and render him obedience, or we shall make war on you, kill you...[or] put you into slavery!'"[4]

The Bible Was Missing

The indigenous people may have "converted," but what was missing in Latin America was any reforming movement. This hindered their development for centuries. The biggest impediment to blessing and freedom in Latin America was the absence of the Word of God. Unlike the Reformers of Europe, the earliest missionaries in the New World didn't encourage the people to read the Bible for themselves. They followed the dictates of the Council of Trent, which officially took the Bible out of people's hands, saying they should rely on the Church and its representatives to judge the "true sense and interpretation of the holy Scriptures."[5]

Of course, many good missionaries sought to serve the people, such as those depicted in the movie *The Mission*. Franciscans, Dominicans, and men like Bartolomé de Las Casas poured themselves out in love for the indigenous people. But the prevailing cruelty of the early conquerors sowed a hateful legacy throughout Latin America. Las Casas told of a native chief in Cuba named Hatuey, whom the governor commanded to be burned alive. They asked Chief Hatuey if he wanted to accept Christianity before his death. Hatuey asked, "Will I find the white man in heaven?" When they said yes, the chief said, "Then I will not be a Christian, for I would not again go to a place where I must find men so cruel!"[6]

Mixing Christianity with Paganism

When you read these heartbreaking accounts, it's little wonder that the subjugated people found ways to hold on to their old beliefs. But that is the second great impediment to Latin America's development—syncretism, the mixture of the gospel with pagan practices. Many Latins are not practicing the truth of Jesus at all. They're practicing *Christo-paganism*, a mixture of things from the Bible and things from their past.

Ancient gods are worshiped alongside Christian saints, sometimes as a blend of an old god and a familiar church figure. For many, shamans and spiritual healers command a place equal to or greater than the clergy. New Year's Eve in Rio de Janeiro is a vivid example. Thousands of Christians gather on the beach to offer sacrifices of fruit, food, expensive perfume, liquor, and cash to spirit beings, setting their gifts adrift in tiny boats.

I've even heard of clergy who keep their feet in both worlds, trying to combine Christianity with Macumba or other spiritist practices. It's common for Brazilians to attend a ritual at night, inviting demonic spirits to take possession of them, then show up for Mass the next morning.

I know this behavior grieves many priests and nuns. The Bible forbids all such practices. They are works of darkness. Truth sets people free, but deception always leads to bondage. It also leads to perpetual poverty, fear, and ignorance.

Despite these things that have stifled progress for centuries, the good news is, Latin America is changing very rapidly. Bondage is giving way to a freedom of God's Spirit in these countries.

Chapter 25

Winds of the Spirit
in Latin America

In the past few decades, some of the most dramatic growth of biblical faith in the world has taken place in Latin America. When you look at the thrilling numbers, they're almost hard to believe. But I have seen the growth happening in country after country throughout the region.

Take Brazil, for example. At the beginning of the twentieth century, Gunnar Vingren and Daniel Berg arrived in Belem, a city at the mouth of the Amazon River. These two young Swedes had been deeply influenced by the Azuza Street movement.[1] As they began to preach to the mostly illiterate poor of that city, thousands began to respond. In just one day, on November 19, 1910, Vingren and Berg stood in the blistering sun, with the temperature 100 degrees Fahrenheit and humidity over 95 percent, to help baptize more than fifty thousand.[2] Think of it! That's more than sixteen times the number baptized on the day of Pentecost.[3]

This launched a movement that has grown to include more than seventeen million in one denomination alone, the Assemblies of God of Brazil,[4] plus millions more in other Pentecostal denominations and in nondenominational charismatic churches and non-charismatic evangelical churches.

Or consider Chile. The first time I went there, in 1961, I visited the Methodist Pentecostal Church in Santiago, Chile. They told me it was the biggest Protestant congregation in the world at that time, with 160,000 members. I stood in their grand auditorium one day and marveled at the sight of six hundred guitars lined up against the wall, waiting for their next worship service.

Throughout Latin America, the number of evangelicals, Pentecostals, and charismatics has continued to mushroom, reaching 151 million in 1990. By 2000, they numbered 181 million.[5]

A Book He'd Never Seen

How has this spectacular growth happened? Mainly, it has come as leaders turned to the Word of God, then taught it to their people. For example, recently I was in Mexico City, about to speak at a large church founded by Pastor Vega. After I taught eight hundred of his leaders, I was about to go into their large auditorium for the Sunday-morning service. As I waited offstage with Pastor Vega, I asked him to tell me his story.

"It's very simple," he said. "I was a layman, a leader in my church. I'd always been an avid reader, sometimes reading several books a week."

Someone gave him a Bible. "I'd never seen one in my life!" he said. He started reading it. When he finished, he realized he hadn't understood it, so he started reading it again. Slowly. "Then it began to open to me."

He got together with some friends. Eight of them began to read the Bible. They studied it, then applied it in their lives.

"We kept on doing that," Pastor Vega said. "Now there are eleven thousand in our church."

The growth of Pastor Vega's church and thousands more like it is spilling over to other continents as these churches send out missionaries. At a Latin American conference called the Cooperación Misionera Iberoamericana (COMIBAM) in São Paulo, Brazil, in 1987, they declared: "We are no longer a mission field, we are now a mission force."[6] They had 1,635 Latin American missionaries working cross-culturally in 1987 when they made that declaration. Now that number has jumped to 8,000, working in 150 nations.[7]

Going to the Hardest Places

In our own mission, we have seen several thousand young Latin YWAMers volunteer. They're going to the hardest places, too. They're willing to live in primitive and dangerous situations. They are bold and daring and love Jesus with all their hearts.

Is all this growth and vitality having an effect on the social fabric of their countries? Yes. It's been clear for some time that Latin America is changing. David Martin, a retired sociology professor from the London School of Economics, has written about the explosive growth of evangelicals in Latin America, particularly among charismatics and Pentecostals, and the transformation that has accompanied it.[8] It's not a complete transformation yet, but a different society is emerging.

Changing before Our Eyes

Martin shows how the gospel message is empowering those on the fringes. Just as in Hauge's peasant movement in Norway, the South American poor are learning how to turn away from harmful habits, how to communicate effectively, and sometimes, even how to read. They are learning to uphold one another and to discipline their energies and their finances. Martin credits their Bible beliefs for their social and economic gains.[9] Slowly they are building the middle class, improving themselves as they apply principles from the Word of God.

Tom Wheaton, a retired missionary to Brazil, tells of an individual in his church who illustrates the transformation going on throughout Latin America. The man and his family live in Belo Horizonte, Brazil's third largest city. In the past they had barely survived. The father had a hard time holding down a job, and his family often went hungry. Every week he squandered what little he had gambling on soccer games and going out drinking and womanizing. But when the man came to Christ, all this changed. He began to learn the Word of God and apply it, and he became a steady worker. Although he still didn't make a lot of money, his salary now went for the family needs—food, clothing, and shoes for the children. The family even moved into a somewhat better house. As the father learned how to live by The Book, the whole family was blessed.

Wheaton says he saw this same thing take place with several men in his congregation. It's a snapshot of what is happening all over Central and South America. Faithfulness and integrity are paying off for thousands and thousands of believers who are working themselves into a better life. These believers are also creating a better society as a result.

I have seen Latin America changing before my eyes as I have made repeated visits for more than fifty years. I used to see unstable governments. One tinhorn dictator would be overthrown by another, who would last awhile only to be replaced by still another. Corruption was the norm; leaders went in poor but always came out rich. Despite resources of oil, precious metals, and gems, the economy of Latin American countries was always fragile, with a privileged few ruling over huge numbers of impoverished people. Now it is changing.

In 1992, something truly remarkable occurred: both President Fernando Collor de Melo of Brazil and President Carlos Andrés Pérez of Venezuela were charged with corruption and removed from office. How could this be when such practices had always been considered *normal* in Latin American countries? The Word of God was being discovered and applied in everyday life. Take Chile for example. Now anyone who tries to bribe a police officer will be arrested. This is not to say that corruption has disappeared from Latin America. But public expectations are changing. Just as in South Korea, now there is a law that is above the leaders of the land.

And I've noticed something else. By 1993, the dictators of Latin America were gone. As I write this, every nation, with the exception of Cuba, has a freely elected president. There are great challenges—not every leader of Latin America is just and fair. We've seen some recent setbacks in stability and freedom, such as when the president of Venezuela expelled scores of missionaries.[10] We may lose some battles like this, but overall victory is coming quickly. The growth of biblical belief in Latin America is continuing at a pace no one can stop. The transformation of Latin America is far from complete but it is well under way.

Part 5

Bringing God's Book
to the Whole World

Chapter 26

Set Your Sights
on the World

When I was a small boy back in the 1940s, I heard that we
were supposed to get the gospel to every nation. I thought
and thought about how we could do that. Then I got an idea. If we
could just go to the moon and find some big black rocks, we could
write a Scripture verse up there for the whole world to read!

But which verse? John 3:16 would be too long. I figured those
rocks would be heavy, and we shouldn't try to move too many of
them. So I finally found a Bible verse short enough: "God is love."[1]
I was sure we could write that in black rocks on the moon so that
everyone on earth could read it.

I smile now at my childish idea of writing on the moon. Even
if it were possible, not everyone understands English, and hundreds
of millions don't read at all. But the goal of reaching the entire
world with the gospel has never left me.

I still think about the same kind of thing. How can we make
sure everyone hears the Good News? How can we make an impact
on all the nations of the world—nations like Japan and those of

Africa and Latin America? How can we transform whole societies, our own and those that are far away?

Jesus called all his followers to be nation builders. He told us to go into all the world and make disciples of all nations.[2] Nation builders may go out as missionaries in the traditional sense, or they may go as led of the Lord into specific occupations to apply God's Word there, as Vories did in Japan.

Many nation builders don't leave their home countries. Instead they apply God's truth in their vocations—in business, government, education, the media, or one of the other spheres of society. Others pray and give support to those who go out. And because the family is the building block of any society, perhaps the most important nation builders are parents who raise their children according to the principles of the Bible. The bottom line is that anyone committed to obeying Jesus by praying, giving, going, and communicating—anyone striving to see his will done on earth as it is in heaven—is part of this worldwide effort to disciple nations.

However, we especially need people who are willing to go to other countries as missionaries—that is, as *sent ones*.[3] We need missionaries because often the amount of darkness is profound. It takes someone who will go in carrying the light. We've seen the darkness in India in the latter part of the eighteenth century when William Carey arrived there. The darkness was just as great when John Wesley began preaching in England or when Calvin went to Geneva. And areas of deep darkness remain in our world now, in the twenty-first century.

Righteous Change, Globally

Jesus came to save all people, to see every nation changed. No matter what country we're from, we must focus on the entire world. These days many are talking about globalization. But the one who first emphasized globalization was God himself when he told Abraham that his offspring would bless all the nations of the world.[4] Jesus told his followers to go into all the world and make disciples of all nations, to go to the ends of the earth.[5] He expects his people to establish righteous, biblical principles *globally*.

Since 1974, when Billy Graham called leaders of the body of Christ together in Lausanne, Switzerland, for the Congress on World Evangelization, the church has been working at a greater intensity to fulfill the Great Commission. Mission leaders have made several attempts to quantify the task—to find where the least-evangelized are. But after more than three decades, no one really knew how much of the job remained to be done. As Dr. Ralph Winter of the U.S. Center for World Mission said, "We *must* know what is happening out there."[6]

4K Omega Zones

David Hamilton, assistant to the president of YWAM's University of the Nations, has laid out the best description yet of what needs to be done. A team of leaders and researchers with technical expertise from such groups as Global Mapping International[7] has pulled together a new framework for seeing the needs of the world. Called 4K, it divides the world into omega zones. The 4K includes global demographics from Christian researchers, the *Encyclopedia Britannica*, the *World Christian Encyclopedia*, the United Nations, and census data from individual countries. As David says, "It will help missionary groups and churches *see where we are not*, to focus on areas of greatest need."

Why do we call it 4K? Because it divides the world into about 4,000 units of similar population size. Each unit is called an "omega zone" because we want every person in every omega zone of the world to fully know Jesus, "the Alpha and the Omega." And since omega is the final letter of the Greek alphabet, we hope this new framework will help mobilize believers for a final push to finish the Great Commission.

The 4K divides the world according to known geopolitical boundaries. Of the 238 sovereign nations and dependent countries of the world, 103 have fewer than three million people. Each of these smaller countries, such as Jamaica, represents one omega zone. But large countries are broken down into smaller units, such as states or provinces and their subdivisions, forming many omega zones. India, for example, is divided into 653 omega zones.

These omega zones are meant to draw attention to the areas of the world with the least presence of the gospel—the spiritually darkest. So areas with easy access to the Word of God, such as urban sections of Brazil, have more people included in an omega zone—up to nine million. A zone with moderate access to the gospel, such as Kenya, will have up to six million. Places with the least access to God's Word, such as Iran, will have no more than three million people per omega zone. This will help attract missions effort to the places that need it most.

Each omega-zone file includes maps and scores of demographic data—showing physical and spiritual needs in an integrated way. You can find such specifics as literacy rates, availability of pure water, unreached people groups, and much more. This data allows leaders to pray and plan for strategies to demonstrate God's character in each omega zone. The 4K team will monitor progress, giving updated information to any groups working to disciple nations. Everything is pointed to one thing—finding where people are still waiting for God's Word.[8]

Put the Bible into Their Hands

We've already seen the effect on nations such as Norway and South Korea as believers have given The Book to more people. We need to do whatever is necessary to get the Bible into every omega zone. According to Wycliffe Bible Translators, 93 percent of the world already have the Bible translated into their mother tongues.[9] But that doesn't mean missionaries have gone and given God's Word to those 93 percent. Just because the Bible exists in their language in a warehouse somewhere doesn't mean that the people have it in their hands or that they have been discipled in its truth.

A Haunting Question

Putting the Bible in everyone's hands has been my dream for a very long time, ever since I was a boy and thought of writing God's Word on the moon. I know we can get his Book to everyone.

When I was a young man, God gave me a dramatic example of how we could put his Word in people's hands. It was 1967, and I was with a YWAM convoy traveling through Mexico to Central

America. We had stopped in a dusty Mexican town to repair a flat tire. While some worked on that, the rest of us delivered a Gospel of John to every home, then held an open-air preaching service.

After our meeting a woman in a faded red dress came up to me. My Spanish wasn't very good, but I understood her to say, "There's no place in my town to get a Bible, and there aren't any in the towns around here. Do you have a Bible in my language?"

I managed to find a Spanish Bible for her. She grasped it to her chest. "¡Muchísimas gracias, señor!"

As we drove away, the woman's question continued to haunt me. *Do you have a Bible in my language?* Then, a picture suddenly came before my eyes—I believe it was what the Bible calls a "vision." I saw a big truck— not a semi, but more like a large moving van. Painted on the side was, *Sólo los deshonestos temen la verdad. Santa Biblia, gratis.*

I didn't know Spanish well enough to *think* in the language, so seeing these sentences was a complete surprise. I translated them slowly in my mind. They meant, "Only the dishonest fear the truth. Free Bibles." What an exciting thought! The phrase "Only the dishonest fear the truth" was completely new to me, and it rang in my mind. It was especially pertinent at that time, as communists were spreading their cause across Latin America.

As the vision continued, I saw young people standing in the back of the truck handing Bibles into eager hands as fast as they could.

While the exact fulfillment of that vision hasn't happened yet, we've been involved in several Bible-distribution projects. Immediately after our experience in that town, when we arrived in Mexico City, I went to the Bible Society and found out how many copies they would let me have. Then I phoned friends and raised the money, buying fifty thousand New Testaments. Our teams distributed them on various university campuses in the city. Over the next few years, our workers were able to place New Testaments in every home in scores of villages and towns, in several states of Mexico. We felt good about that, but God had greater challenges— and excitement—ahead for us.

Chapter 27

Getting Bibles Out There

Soon another Bible-distribution project, accomplished with breathtaking speed, would have some of the longest-lasting results. And it all happened so easily.

We were in Europe in the 1970s. It was a time of social upheaval with protests against the Vietnam War and with much drug abuse, even among U.S. soldiers on army bases. Our teams were working as guests of U.S. Army chaplains, trying to reach many American troops in Germany.

One day in 1972, in a YWAM school in Lausanne, Switzerland, we broke into small groups for intercessory prayer. In my small group we asked the Lord what he wanted us to pray for, since that was our practice. Several of us had the same impression—to intercede for U.S. troops at military bases in Germany. We could have just prayed, "God, bless the army guys. Save them!" Instead we asked the Lord for specific items to pray for.

I had an idea: *ask for 100,000 Bibles to give out to all the soldiers.* That seemed far-fetched, but I prayed it aloud, asking the Lord for 100,000 Bibles and for them to be delivered.

I knew Colonel Jim Ammerman, the head chaplain for the V Corps Army—all the U.S. troops in Germany. In fact, he and his wife had recently visited us in Lausanne. I thought he might be part of the answer to our prayers. So our small group prayed for God to prepare the Ammermans, in case they were to be part of this plan.

Another thought came to me in the prayer time: *contact Dr. Kenneth Taylor*. I had heard of him. He was the one who published *The Living Bible*. He was also the founder of Tyndale House Publishers. I wondered how I could get ahold of him. Again a thought came: *ask Brother Andrew. That's a good idea*, I thought. Brother Andrew was a friend of mine, a brave Dutch believer who had been distributing Bibles in closed countries. I'd contact him.

But first, it was time for us to join the others, where each group would share what happened in their prayer time. When we told the rest of the school what we had prayed—for 100,000 Bibles to give out to the American soldiers in Germany—a hum of excitement went around the room. How would we see this happen?

A Bible Airlift

Later that day I phoned Brother Andrew. "Do you know how I could meet Dr. Kenneth Taylor?" I asked.

Brother Andrew helped me locate Dr. Taylor, who happened to be in Europe that week. I phoned him in Athens. He was returning to the U.S. but agreed to meet with me the next day during a brief stopover in Germany.

I traveled to Frankfurt and found Dr. Taylor at the airport. I told him about our prayer time and the impression that we were to give 100,000 Bibles to the GIs. He nodded and smiled. "I happen to have 100,000 Bibles left over from a Billy Graham campaign. I'll give them to you for the soldiers if you can get them delivered from the States."

Wow! One hundred thousand free Bibles! But how on earth would we come up with the money to ship them from America to Germany? I knew God was leading, so I kept following one step at a time. In my mind's eye I saw a convoy of trucks delivering Bibles to the U.S. bases in Germany. Yes. It would happen.

That evening I went to the home of Colonel Ammerman outside Frankfurt. He and his wife, Charlene, greeted me at the door. They graciously invited me to stay for dinner and spend the night. While Charlene cooked up a wonderful meal, I broached the topic.

"Sir, we've been praying about Bibles for your soldiers." I took a breath. "In the Spirit, I saw a convoy of trucks delivering Bibles to the U.S. military bases in Germany."

I paused. The colonel received these strange words rather calmly, but his eyes sparkled. "Wonderful! Go on."

"These were complete Bibles."

The colonel nodded. "Yes."

"One hundred thousand Living Bibles." Then I told him about the offer from Kenneth Taylor.

Colonel Ammerman leaned forward. "Loren, you have heard from God, exactly, on all counts. I've been praying for Bibles to give to our troops—the full Bible in an easy-to-understand translation."

But what about the shipping? He said he would take care of it. Colonel Ammerman arranged for the military to take two planeloads of Bibles to Germany. When the project was introduced among the leaders at Tyndale Publishing, one of their editors, Wendell Hawley, recognized the name of Jim Ammerman. It turned out Hawley just happened to have served under Ammerman as his supervisory chaplain in Vietnam. Tyndale ended up paying for the shipping of the rest of the Bibles to Germany. The trucks arrived at the various locations of the V Corps Army, delivering their precious cargo just as the Lord had shown me in the vision.

Every soldier who wanted a copy got one. And since thousands of GIs came through there each month before heading to Vietnam, Korea, or other parts of the world, it wasn't long before every one of the 100,000 Bibles had been put into soldiers' hands all over the world. Colonel Ammerman even set up oral Bible readings over the army public address systems in Germany to call attention to the offer of free Bibles.

Years later, Colonel and Mrs. Ammerman attended my father's funeral. Afterward, I sat talking with them. Colonel Ammerman said that the Bible distribution led to one of the greatest moves of

God he had ever seen. Many GIs became believers while reading those Bibles. Some became missionaries. Mrs. Ammerman added that before, they hadn't known any top military officers who were dedicated followers of Jesus. "Now there are many," she said, "and we trace it back to the Bible distribution."

Only eternity will reveal the full impact of what began with a handful of young people praying that day in a small room of a YWAM school in Switzerland.

Saturating Hawaii with the Word

The Bible is indeed The Book that transforms nations—but only if the people of the nations have access to it and apply it in their lives. Believers in the gospel of Jesus Christ are responsible for taking it to those who don't have it. We also need to restore The Book in places where it has been lost. People must have the chance to hear and obey God's Word.

In 1983, President Ronald Reagan proclaimed The Year of the Bible in America. Dr. Bill Bright of Campus Crusade for Christ headed up the national program, asking me to chair the effort in Hawaii, the state where I lived at the time.

Just prior to this, the Lord had told me not to travel outside the Hawaiian Islands during 1983. I had traveled extensively in ministry every year since 1954, but I was to stay in the state during 1983. I saw why when Bill Bright invited me to head up this exciting effort in the islands.

Hawaii has a smaller percentage of believers than most American states. One out of nine homes is Buddhist. And large numbers of people whose mother tongue is not English live in the islands. This presented a formidable challenge.

We decided on a strategy of tying Bible distribution to a historic theme. We printed a commemorative edition of the New Testament with a painting by Steve Regas on the cover. The painting portrayed the *Thaddeus,* the ship that brought the first missionaries to Kona in 1820. In the background was Mokuaikaua Church, the first congregation established in Hawaii. A twelve-page section in the back of the Bible told of the arrival of the first missionaries and the history of the church in Hawaii. This true story helped counteract certain works of fiction that slandered the early missionaries and twisted the real history of the islands.

Preachers, Priests, and a Rabbi

Protestant and Catholic church officials endorsed the delivery of these New Testaments to every home in Hawaii. With the leadership of a rabbi, Old Testaments were delivered to Jewish families. Residents of the state speak fifteen languages. So we did research to find out how many Testaments of which language to take to each neighborhood.

Almost every denomination took part in the program. More than six thousand volunteers helped take the New Testament in an appropriate language to every home in the islands. We saturated the entire state with the Word of God. And almost everyone was glad to receive his or her New Testament.

What came out of the Year of the Bible? I can't prove it scientifically, but more than twenty years later, I can see the difference in Hawaii. When we came here in the seventies, there were no large churches. The biggest was a congregation of a few hundred in Honolulu. On our island, only a few churches were preaching the gospel, and those were lightly attended. Back in the early nineteenth century, a major revival spread through the Hawaiian Islands. The largest church in the world at that time was on the Big Island of Hawaii. But those revival fires had long since cooled into indifference.

Now, as I write this, several vibrant congregations in the islands have memberships in the thousands. Within five years of the Year of the Bible, the number of churches preaching the gospel in the Kona area, where I live, rose to twenty-six. Thousands of short-term and hundreds of long-term missionaries are trained and sent from Kona all over Asia and the rest of the world. Hawaii has become a lighthouse in the Pacific. And I believe the Bible saturation of 1983 played a key role.

Chapter 28

On the Cutting Edge

The Bible, together with God's Spirit, can transform any nation on earth. We need to put this belief into action. Did you know that if every Bible-believing person gave less than $10, we could provide Bibles for every home in the world?[1] Believers already have the manpower and the money to deliver the Bible in an appropriate language to every home on earth. What are we waiting for?

Of course, such a program would require cultural sensitivity. We'd need to tailor methods of Bible distribution to the needs of each target population, as we did in the Year of the Bible in Hawaii. And we should precede the Bible giveaway by announcing what we're about to do. We could say, "We're offering a very important gift to every home in our community—a copy of The Book that blesses nations."

After the delivery of the Bible itself, we could offer programs to teach people how to read and understand it. Again, we'd have to fit these plans to the needs of specific populations. Bible teachers could be ready to provide free classes for those who want to know more. Bruce Wilkinson, author of *The Prayer of Jabez* and founder of Walk through the Bible, is establishing WorldTeach, the largest Bible-teaching faculty in the world. Its goal is to train 120,000 Bible teachers—one for every 50,000 people on earth.[2]

What could be more important? We must give the world culturally relevant methods of studying and understanding The Book. As we do this we will transform lives and raise up nation builders.

The Bible, Coming to a Pub Near You

God's people have used mass Bible distribution to great effect. Another way to get the Word out is to have public reading of God's Word. Let me give you a recent example.

It's Saturday afternoon in a pub in Perth, Australia. Three YWAM students are seated in a booth, sipping soft drinks. After a quiet prayer, a young woman begins reading her Bible aloud, in a normal speaking voice.

"The Spirit of the Sovereign Lord is on me, because the Lord has anointed me to preach good news to the poor..."

As she continues, her reading becomes a soft sound throughout the pub. Locals and tourists look up from their drinks or food, puzzled at first, then listening.

"...to comfort all who mourn, and provide for those who grieve in Zion..."

"Uh, excuse me, miss," a man at a nearby booth says. "What are you doing?"

"Oh, we're students from a Bible school. Part of our course is to read the Bible out loud. Because we love to read the Bible, we want to share it with others," she explains, and continues reading aloud.

Some might think people would consider this an intrusion. But in almost every instance the public has reacted positively. According to Debbie Hicks from Australia, it happens like this every weekend. Debbie has launched more than fifty YWAM Schools of Biblical Studies (SBS) in Sweden, Nepal, India, Switzerland, Barbados, Japan, Australia, England, France, South Africa, Malaysia, Ukraine, and the United States. Every Saturday, she requires her SBS students to find a place to read the Bible aloud in public.

The students have read aloud in cafés, bars, parks, even the zoo. They're told not to use a PA system, but neither are they to mumble the words. They read in clinics, among the homeless, and on buses and ferries. They've even read the Bible aloud while riding camels among tourists in the outback of Australia.

Some passersby ignore the reading; others can't believe anyone would read the Bible out loud in public. In some cases people sit down to listen or even take a turn reading aloud themselves. In rare cases people react negatively—mostly in universities. I find it interesting that universities are some of the least tolerant places on earth, with little freedom of speech and thought.

Most of the time people respond positively. Maybe it's the power of the Word of God. When students finish reading the Bible passage, they ask the listeners, "Do you have any questions about what I've read?" Often people do have questions, and sometimes they give their hearts to the Lord.

Bible-Reading Marathons

Another way to get God's Word into the public is to arrange a Bible-reading marathon. With this method it's important to get permission to use a public setting. A public-address system will help, too. Also, alert the media ahead of time. It takes only seventy-two hours to read the entire Bible aloud, cover to cover. Or you could choose to read the Word only during daylight hours. It takes about a week to get through the entire Bible this way. If the reading were done in a park, people could come during their lunch hour and listen to the Word. Such marathons attract public interest in the Bible.

In Ancient Times...

There's scriptural precedent for public Bible reading. At a crucial time in Jewish history, Ezra read God's Word in its entirety at a public gathering. The story is told in Nehemiah, chapter 8. This group of Israelites had returned from Babylonian captivity to rebuild the temple and the city of Jerusalem. But their personal lives were also in shambles. Ezra read aloud to them from dawn until noon the first day. Public reading continued for another six days. The people repented, and spiritual revival broke out.

The New Testament also speaks of public Bible reading. Paul told Timothy to pay attention to public reading of Scripture.[3]

...And Down at Wal-Mart

Such examples aren't restricted to Bible times. Recently more than fifty teens in Ephrata, Pennsylvania, obtained permission to hold a Bible-reading marathon in front of a Wal-Mart SuperCenter. Beginning at 3:00 PM and running until midnight of the next day, the teens and church volunteers read the Bible nonstop over a PA system. Nobody complained. Instead, several customers asked the management if the young people could do it again the next year.[4]

Smuggling One Million Bibles

Our job is to take The Book to everyone. Operation Mobilisation (OM),[5] Scripture Union,[6] the United Bible Societies,[7] and Brother Andrew's Open Doors[8] have done many things to distribute Bibles. In one night alone in 1981, Open Doors volunteers smuggled one million Bibles into China in what they called Project Pearl.[9] At tremendous personal risk, underground church leaders received the books and carried them to every province.

Local police in one area of southern China captured men carrying one thousand of the Project Pearl Bibles. They jailed the couriers, then threw God's Word into an open cesspool. The men were released from jail a few days later. They waited until nightfall, then climbed down into the cesspool, retrieving every one of the foul-smelling Bibles. They washed them off carefully, sprayed them with perfume, and carried them to believers.

That was twenty-five years ago. God's Book is still a "pearl of great price," worthy of any risk or personal sacrifice. We need to find new ways to get Bibles out to people, especially to countries where the law forbids God's Book. We must ask the Lord for a wave of fresh thinking.

Exploiting New Technology

There are multitudes of ways to get God's Word out, and our creative God is always releasing innovative means. New technology, paired with Scripture, can change the world. Some years ago I noticed something as I studied the history of God's people. Often, a new technology came just prior to a new release of God's message. For instance:

- The invention of the first alphabet came in time for God's Word to be put down in Scripture.
- The technology of the printing press arrived at just the right time to allow the Reformers to place the Bible and biblical teaching into the hands of the people.
- People discovered electronic means of mass communication—radio and film—as the evangelical movement was being born, allowing believers to use these means of spreading the Word.
- TV and satellite transmission were developed just as the charismatic and Jesus People revivals were beginning, allowing all kinds of gospel television to spread around the world.

And now the Internet has burst upon the scene, influencing all of us. Yes, some people are using it to do terrible things. Pornography, gambling, racist ideologies, and even terrorist activities are poisoning millions through the Internet. But I believe God allowed the Internet to be invented so that his people can use it in our final push to reach the whole world.

With the release of the Internet and accompanying technology, we can do things we haven't imagined until now. I don't know all the ways God's people will use the Internet to spread his Word, but I have seen some new things emerging.

At the 2000 Summer Olympics in Sydney and at the 2002 Winter Olympics in Salt Lake City, YWAMers distributed Bibles on CDs. Imagine—the entire Bible in more than forty languages on one CD!

Why don't we take that a step further? We could use the Internet to provide a digital version for every language translation of the Bible. How many techies would it take to get those translations online so that billions could find the Bible in their own languages?

Can't you see the possibilities?

Downloading Arabic Bibles by the Thousands

At least eighty-five ministries are already using the Internet in innovative ways to reach people in the Middle East, North Africa, and the Arabian Peninsula, according to Strategic Resource

Group.[10] Despite attempts from some governments to block these websites, one organization has forty-two thousand visitors every day. Another reports more than two thousand Arabic Bibles are being downloaded each month. [11] One group says they're seeing twenty people a month come to Christ online.[12] Since more than half of the population in the Middle East is under twenty-five, and youth are more computer savvy than their elders, many of these new Arabic converts are young people.[13]

We're living in such a tremendous time of opportunity!

As followers of Jesus, we have the responsibility of carrying God's message to every people group on the earth, teaching them everything he taught us. Faithful men and women have been pursuing this task for centuries. Countless lives have been changed, as well as whole societies. Just think of all that our forerunners accomplished with so few tools at their disposal. Think what it meant to preserve and share God's Word when they had to painstakingly copy every word of it by hand—for *every single copy!* And imagine carrying the gospel to a new area when you had to *walk* (or, if you were really fortunate, ride a horse or a mule) thousands of miles over rough and dangerous roads to get there. Throughout the centuries, there have been new languages to learn, sometimes even written language forms to create, and much translation to be done. Those who went before us paid a great price and accomplished so much.

Today a vast array of tools makes our job easier. Some places are still isolated. It's difficult or even dangerous to travel to certain areas. Language challenges still confront us. But we can reach most people who need God's Word rather quickly and easily with modern transportation. We can use many new forms of communications technology. And instead of handwritten Scriptures, which were bulky, expensive, and rare, we can mass produce God's Word in a compact, easily handled form. For the most part, our willingness to obey the Lord and move out is the only real limitation.

If we meet this challenge, countless individuals will find new life and fulfill their God-given destinies. As we reach more and more people, we will find a tipping point in each nation as critical minorities begin to influence their countries. This is the way we will see God's kingdom extended throughout the earth. We can see it happen.

Chapter 29

Reaching the 7 Percent

One Sunday morning just before Christmas, a pastor in a restricted-access country[1] said he was going to read seven verses from the second chapter of Luke.

As he began, something like electricity buzzed across his small congregation. They were hearing the verses in their mother tongue for the first time! Wycliffe's SIL translators and a local team had just finished providing that part of the Bible for these people.

The pastor paused and looked up, his heart overflowing. He couldn't stop with the usual end to the familiar Christmas passage. He said, "It tastes so good, it tastes so good!" and kept on reading. Members of the translation team, sitting in front on rough, wooden benches, began to sob. In another part of the congregation, teenage girls stared at one another, then fell into a group hug. When the pastor finished, people cheered and shouted "Amen!" and "Hallelujah!"

Letting the Words Fall over You

Afterward, a doctor in the congregation said she had closed her eyes as her pastor read. "I let the words fall over me. For the first time in my life, I felt washed in the Word. I feel like I've heard [the Christmas story] for the first time."[2]

Shouldn't everyone have the opportunity to let the words fall over them, to be washed in the Word? Yet for 7 percent of the world's people, this isn't possible. They still don't have the Bible translated into their mother tongue. According to Wycliffe, people speaking more than 2,644 languages and dialects are waiting for that.[3] Even though some of them speak and read a second language in which the Bible *is* available, it's important for them to have the Word in their mother tongue. That's their "heart language." It is the language they understand best.

And, of course, others within this 7 percent don't speak a second language. They don't have the Bible at all.

God's Word in Every Tongue

A few years ago I attended a meeting of missions executives. One of the ministries has staff with advanced linguistics degrees working on Bible translation. Their leader asked me, "How can we get more young people involved?"

So I shared what happened at the University of the Nations in Kona, Hawaii. Three tribesmen from a minor tribe of around twenty thousand in Nagaland, in northeast India, were studying on our campus. One day they said to their YWAM teacher, Dr. Ron Smith, "We don't have a Bible in our language—the Khoibu dialect. Can you help us?"

Dr. Smith and these three students, along with two computer experts, picked up the challenge. It took them three years. The result was a Khoibu translation of the New Testament. Dr. Smith estimates that the computer experts saved about ten years of work. They dedicated the completed translation at a church service in Nagaland and ended up giving Khoibu New Testaments to every Khoibu-speaking family.

Speeding Up the Process

In order to produce a Khoibu New Testament, we used computer technologies and students to help speed the process of Bible translation. This is just one example—we need to find new ways to shorten the wait for the 2,644 language groups who still don't have the Bible.

Wycliffe uses linguists with extensive training. But even lay-people can be involved in Bible translation. We need to see entre-preneurial types put their minds to this. What solutions can you find? How can we get more people involved? How can we stream-line the process of Bible translation? We've seen laypeople come up with other creative solutions in recent years—in projects as diverse as Habitat for Humanity building homes for the homeless and food banks getting groceries for the needy. What can we do to pick up the challenge of Bible translation?

Your Church Can Do This

It would take only 2,644 local churches, each adopting one language group to complete this part of the Great Commission.[4] Volunteers from a church could raise the money and go meet with people from one of these 2,644 language groups—where they'll usually find at least a couple of people who also speak English. Representatives—maybe two or three from the language group—could listen to English tapes of the Bible in a suitable modern ver-sion. The native speakers could listen verse by verse, discuss it, and record an oral translation into their mother tongue phrase by phrase. Volunteers from the adoptive church could be there to facilitate the process, helping, praying, even bringing them glasses of water. If local missionaries couldn't find believers to work in this process, they could use unbelievers. After all, translating the Bible verse by verse would likely win many of them to Christ.

Once these tribal volunteers exhausted their ideas about the text, another group who speaks the same language or dialect could come in. Members of the second group would listen to the record-ing the first group made. Then they would translate the text back into English. This would help volunteers from the adoptive church catch any unclear or misleading translation. You would probably want to repeat one or two more cycles of this process to make sure the translation is accurate. Volunteers from the adoptive church could even spell one another, staying overseas only a few weeks at a time to see the project along.

Afterward, these oral translations could be presented to a group such as Wycliffe to help in their ministry of providing written Bible translations. This sort of thing would never replace the work of missionary linguists. But it could complement what they're doing, fill in the gaps, and help to speed up the process.

Could your church do this? YWAM and Global Recordings are already doing oral book translations in a similar way in the Amazon. It is a tedious process, but it works. It could be done elsewhere, producing oral Bibles for each language group. Rather than taking years, as it does when translators have to create an alphabet and written language to produce a written Bible, each of these oral Bibles could be produced in a matter of months. We might not prefer an oral Bible ourselves. But listeners from cultures without a written language are very skilled at retaining what they hear. And many are not able to read and can only receive the Word orally. And what's most important, they would have God's Word in their heart language.

School in the Jungle

Another way to streamline the process of Bible translation is to train translators out in the field. Bráulia Ribeiro, a Brazilian YWAM leader, is a trained, experienced linguist. She is working with fifteen tribal groups in the Amazon, each with its own distinct language. She teaches a course on basic linguistics and phonetics there at our YWAM center in the jungle. Anyone who wants to can come and get trained.[5] Introductory classes in these topics can be taken at a university, of course. But imagine learning these skills *in the field*, tailored specifically to the needs of Bible translation, with immediate real-life demonstration and application! Interns could do these first translations as oral Bibles. Translation experts could use these recordings later to develop a written form.

Anointed Gadgets

How would people hear these translations? An oral translation could be mass-produced on dependable, long-lasting CDs or DVDs. Or they could be produced at a much lower technological level. Global Recordings has invented various devices to play without electricity, even hand-cranked players.[6]

Ken Crowell, CEO of Galtronics in Israel, has developed MegaVoice, a line of handheld audio devices that need no tapes or CDs. They're the size and thickness of several credit cards. They have no moving parts and are self-contained, water-resistant, and rugged. This unique system plays only the message programmed onto a microchip embedded in the unit which cannot be erased or changed without using the MegaVoice secure message-handling system. Solar-powered with rechargeable batteries, the unit can also be played or recharged off a 9-volt plug adapter. It can be used for individual listening or with a small group. One of the MegaVoices, the Ambassador, has the capacity to store the entire Bible on one unit. Other applications for the MegaVoice line are in development.[7]

Telling the Story

Focusing on oral teaching also makes sense for reasons other than speeding Bible translation.

One "new" strategy for reaching people is as old as Adam and Eve. Since the dawn of humanity people passed on their history, as well as values and information, by telling stories.

When Jesus was on earth, an estimated 93 percent of the world's people learned orally. That's why he used storytelling to show them who God was and how he wanted them to live.

Today missionaries in the "orality" movement are following Jesus' example to reach the lost. The majority of those who've never heard the gospel—70 percent—are either functionally or totally illiterate.[8] New Tribes Mission first developed a method of chronological Bible "storying" in Papau New Guinea in the 1970s. Now YWAM, Campus Crusade for Christ, Wycliffe/SIL, Trans World Radio, and the International Mission Board of the Southern Baptist Convention are using this form of storytelling to reach entire communities who are more accustomed to learning by listening.[9]

The best way to explain how orality missionaries work is to share what's happening on one of the teams right now. One of our YWAMers named Sarah and five young recruits from other mission agencies are deep in preparation in one of Europe's capital cities. They will leave soon for a limited access country to live with an unreached people group.

The young people have already learned sixty to eighty stories that cover the Bible from Genesis to Revelation. These stories convey all the basic teachings of God's Word and are designed to lead people to Christ and teach principles for transformation in individuals and in the particular culture. Sarah and her coworkers have studied ahead of time to make sure the stories are culturally appropriate and understandable, and once there, they will search for someone who speaks English to be their interpreter.

The team will tell their stories over a period of time, usually during community gatherings.[10] Since many unreached people groups make decisions as a community rather than as individuals, all of them can be brought along together to a point of faith and understanding. The team will be embedded in the unreached people group for up to a year. Their goal is to see the birth of a fellowship of believers. These believers will memorize the stories so that they can in turn reach others.

This one example shows what's going on in many places. I'm sure we're going to see a stunning number of new believers within the next few years. As International Orality Network president Avery Willis says, "Stories serve as bridges, remove barriers, and fill in gaps to make the gospel fully alive and relevant to the listeners."[11]

As important as the orality missions are to reach people for Christ and transform their communities, we also know that people need to learn how to read in order to reach their full potential. Nearly one in six of the world's people is illiterate.[12] When functional literacy is considered, the number is even larger. What else can be done to help these people know God's Word for themselves?

An Amazing Shortcut to Reading

I see God's hand in all kinds of technological releases and developments. I sense he is cheering us on, allowing people to make discoveries to smooth the way before us, to take his Word to every person on earth. One of the most exciting breakthroughs is a simple writing system that can teach anyone how to read in his or her language in only two weeks.

I know that's hard to believe. How can you teach a totally illiterate person how to read in two weeks? But it's true. It's like a phonics system on steroids, hundreds of times easier and faster to understand. This new technique came from Dr. Sek Yen Kim-Cho, a Korean linguist and professor who teaches PhD candidates at the State University of New York in Buffalo.[13]

More than thirty years ago, Dr. Kim-Cho prayed all night, asking the Lord what to do with her life. The Lord said he wanted to give her a writing system to help missionaries teach people how to read the Bible.

After thirty years of working on this program, Dr. Kim-Cho invented a global writing system. She named it *nurigeul* after the simplified alphabet created by Korea's King Sejong in the fifteenth century.[14] In a system inspired by her study of King Sejong, she came up with symbols for every sound humans produce in the five areas of the throat and mouth. These sounds are the basis for every language on earth. Dr. Kim-Cho says her tests show that people can learn how to read their own language with only two weeks of instruction, using her system with its quickly grasped symbols.[15]

When Dr. Kim-Cho made her presentation of *nurigeul* at the United Nations Educational, Scientific and Cultural Organization (UNESCO), the delegates gave her a standing ovation. They could see the tremendous potential for development in every nation. And *nurigeul* will be used for the development of the nations: Dr. Kim-Cho told UNESCO that her writing system was primarily for missionaries to teach illiterate people all over the world how to read the Bible.

The Two Mongolias

For those of us who grew up in countries where everyone went to school, it's hard to realize how Dr. Kim-Cho's writing system will liberate people. Take China, for instance. According to Dr. Kim-Cho, experts say the Chinese are 70 percent illiterate, even though official records deny this, saying they are only 10 percent illiterate. Dr. Kim-Cho explains the discrepancy—the Chinese government considers all those who have attended school through the second grade to be literate, whether or not they can actually read and write. Yet it's very difficult to learn Chinese characters. Most students haven't mastered them by second grade. It takes many years for Chinese boys and girls to learn how to read and write.

You can also see the problem when you compare the two Mongolias: Russia controlled Outer Mongolia for years, so its people learned to write their language in Cyrillic letters. But across the border, the Chinese taught people in Inner Mongolia to write their language with Chinese characters. Today, though they speak the same language, Outer Mongolia is 80 percent literate, while Inner Mongolia is only 10 percent literate.[16]

Why is this important? It is critical for a country to have people who can read and write. A nation can never develop if illiteracy is crippling its people. And most important, its people can never read a Bible if they can't read at all.

Powerful Tools in Our Hands

One day I got a phone call in Kona. It was a dear friend of mine, Dr. Kun Mo Chung, calling from Korea. He's the president of a university in Seoul. He told me about Dr. Kim-Cho and her universal writing system. We arranged for her to come to Kona. There, she presented her writing system to me and other leaders of YWAM's University of the Nations. She showed us a Chinese New Testament with *nurigeul*, the global writing system marks, alongside the Chinese characters. We looked at it in wonder. Dr. Kim-Cho used it to teach illiterate Chinese how to read their own mother tongue in *two weeks*. Now Dr. Kim-Cho is offering her system to missionaries to help fulfill the Great Commission.

We have an incredible privilege, just being alive right now. We're about to see the culmination of what believers have pursued for thousands of years. Those who've gone before us long ago and those who have been working very recently have placed powerful tools in our hands. Now it's up to us. We must keep our hearts and minds open—to hear God's call, to receive his guidance and strength, and to seize the opportunities. Always, God is calling us to use our imaginations as much as our wills. We can't be stuck in old ways of doing things. God wants us to see possibilities, to be willing to think of new things and do them by his strength. Because with God, we can do everything.[17]

Part 6

Keeping Our Eyes on God

Chapter 30

The Spirit and the Word

A great prayer movement has been sweeping across the earth in the past thirty years. Intercession for nations and individual people groups is growing, becoming one of the important moves of God in our time. The church is also evangelizing on an unprecedented scale, as well as doing works of mercy for the poor and needy. Added to these good things is the way the Lord's people are rediscovering worship.

However, as I have traveled the nations during the past few decades, I have noticed what is missing. We aren't discipling people in the Word of God. In most churches, from small congregations to the megachurches, we spend an hour—even an hour and a half—singing worship songs. We enjoy it. It's a good thing. But if a preacher takes more than twenty minutes to teach the Word—thirty at the most—people will complain. And for too many, those twenty minutes are all the Bible they're going to get all week long!

It reminds me of a saying from an old friend: "Sermonettes make Christianettes."

We must restore some balance. We need solid Bible teaching *along with* prayer and the life of the Spirit. If we spend time in praise, worship, and intercessory prayer but fail to pursue truth in God's Word, our minds and habits will stay the same—unrenewed. So will the thinking and actions of our countries.

Soaked in Scripture, but Lost

Another danger occupies the opposite end of the spectrum. Some people love to spend time in their Bibles, searching out its treasures. But if they do this without submitting to the Holy Spirit, they fall into another kind of trap. The letter of the Word is not only inadequate—the Bible says that the letter of the Word will kill.[1] There's something known as "bibliolatry," which threatens people on this side of the scale. Bibliolatry is when people put all their hopes and belief in the Bible itself rather than in the Author of its pages. They become known for their theological purity and eventually for their rigidity, legalism, and intolerance. They're unwilling to change their opinions even if the Lord himself tries to get their attention.

The Pharisees were a prime example of this. The religious leaders of Jesus' day were men of the Word. They reverenced Scripture in ways we don't even approach. Every Jewish boy was required to memorize the Pentateuch—the first five books of the Bible—by the age of twelve. The Pharisees knew the Scripture line by line, mark by mark, backward and forward, as well as centuries of rabbinical teaching that supplemented it. They were soaked with Scripture, but they were *lost*. Jesus said they were the blind leading the blind.[2] When they made converts, they duplicated their own spiritual bankruptcy.[3] The Pharisees were proud of their knowledge of Scripture, but they had no idea they were rejecting its Author, who was standing in front of them.

How can we avoid that pitfall? How can we love the Bible and seek out its truth without falling into the trap of religious pride, deception, the letter of the law, and death? We must ask God by his Spirit to open his Word to us. It's the Spirit and the Word together that bring life.[4]

Fiji: A Dramatic Return to Life

Sometimes the life brought by the Spirit and the Word can be quite literal, and utterly amazing. Recently, I had an unusual visit from three representatives of the nation of Fiji to our YWAM University of the Nations campus in Kona, Hawaii. The men were sent on an important errand by the government, the Great Council of Chiefs, and the pastors of Fiji.

We introduced our distinguished guests at a public gathering of eight hundred YWAM staff and students. The men wore Fijian *sulus*—tailored sarongs worn with Western-style shirts. With great dignity they sat cross-legged on the floor of our large pavilion and began to make solemn speeches in typical island fashion. First they honored me by presenting me with a whale's tooth. I learned later that they give out very few of these. Whales' teeth are passed from generation to generation in families of chiefs and royalty. To present a person with one is the highest honor Fijians can give. When they give you a whale's tooth, they are linking you to them and to their history in a deep bond of commitment.

As the men's speeches were translated from Fijian, we learned their purpose in coming. They were asking YWAM's help in fulfilling God's destiny for their nation. Would we come to Fiji and give them more teaching from the Word of God?

For the past few years, Fiji has seen the start of a national awakening. The kind of transformation we've been describing in this book is beginning there. It all began after Fiji went through two violent coups in 2000. Although the authorities put down the rebellion and imprisoned the instigators, the leaders of Fiji felt their country had been diminished in the eyes of the world. Their economy was in trouble. Their youth were going astray. Their country was losing its direction in every category.

A Unique Foot-Washing Meeting

For those unfamiliar with this nation, Fiji is the number one communication, education, and commercial center of the South Pacific (Polynesia and Melanesia). Its population is just over half indigenous Fijian (mostly Christians) and nearly half Indo-Fijian (largely Hindus and Muslims), whose ancestors were brought to Fiji as laborers during the British colonial era.

In recent years, some Fijians began to resent the Indo-Fijians' financial and political successes. In an outbreak of violence in 2000, Fijians looted and burned Indian stores. Insurgents raped Indo-Fijian women and injured many. The violence left eight dead.[5]

During this terrible time for his country, the new prime minister, Laisenia Qarase went to the pastors and godly leaders, asking them to end the quarreling between denominations. He felt that bitterness in the body of Christ had helped lead to the deep national divisions in the country. The spiritual leaders came together, asking one another's forgiveness for malice and slander.

Then Prime Minister Qarase asked the pastors to find out what God wanted the country to do. The church leaders began to fast and pray. The prime minister and the president joined them, also calling for the people of the nation to fast and pray.

After they restored political stability, Prime Minister Qarase organized a gathering in Albert Park in Suva, Fiji's capital. Virtually all the church leaders were there, as were the political leaders. They made formal apologies to the Indo-Fijian community and to the public. Then in a stunning act of public contrition, the prime minister got down on his knees before the opposition leader, Mahendra Chaudhry, a Hindu, and asked his forgiveness. Next, the prime minister reached for a basin and a towel and washed his political opponent's feet.[6]

Hundreds of Fijians followed their prime minister's example that day in Albert Park, going to one another, weeping and asking forgiveness.

Healing the Land

Repentance and restitution didn't stop after that day in Albert Park. Pastors continued to meet together, asking God how to bring healing to their land and how they should advise the government leaders.

As the pastors sought the Lord, they came up with a specific plan. This plan, now being implemented, includes a mobile team of pastors and lay volunteers called Healing the Land. This team is ready to go into any village whose chief invites them. There they fast and pray for a week on-site. Then they visit all the people, going from house to house. They hold Bible teaching every night. The schedule is structured and comprehensive, with teaching on basic subjects and opportunities for the people to respond in repentance and spiritual warfare.

Bill Efinger and a team from YWAM Kona recently went along with the Healing the Land team on one of their visits. They traveled to the village of Saunauka, population five hundred.

Repenting in the Hot Sun

Bill said, "Every night the entire village came out to hear the Bible teaching." After the team thoroughly laid out the conditions for repentance and reconciliation, they gave the people the chance to respond. The entire village made a covenant to serve the Lord Jesus Christ. Everyone. One hundred percent. On Saturday they gathered for a formal time of repentance and reconciliation. All day long they sat cross-legged on the ground in the hot sun. The heads of clans and subclans, their chief, and the people took turns publicly confessing their sins to the community.

"It was dignified, according to island protocol, but we could feel their passion," Bill said. "We were amazed as the interpreters kept us aware of what was being said. The Fijians were making themselves completely transparent, asking forgiveness." A widow confessed she had been living off of money that her late husband had stolen from the church over the years. The athletes of the village—the soccer team, the rugby players, and the volleyball team—got up in front of the community. All the lanky youths stood quietly with their heads bowed as their chosen spokesman asked forgiveness for their rebellion, drunkenness, and disobedience to parents.

George Otis Jr. tells in his documentary *Let the Sea Resound* of similar meetings going on in fourteen villages of Fiji.[7] In one village where their forefathers had killed and eaten a missionary in the nineteenth century, the Fijians were stricken with guilt. They paid for the airfare to fly the victim's descendants in from England so they could ask their forgiveness in person.

In other acts of repentance, marijuana growers uprooted and burned 13,864 plants in the highlands of Fiji, worth an estimated eleven million dollars. A leader in the reconciliation movement,

Savenaca Nakauyaca, says, "They realized they were guilty of defiling the land and under God's curse, [so they] gave up drug farming and gave their hearts to God."[8]

Others have abandoned witchcraft rituals passed on from their forefathers. Bill Efinger told of watching the villagers of Saunaka burn all their idols and articles of witchcraft in a large field.

All of this process has been saturated with Bible teaching. The Healing the Land team holds intensive Bible studies in converted villages, showing them how to live their lives personally and as a group.

As the people have repented and started living rightly, God has brought literal life back to their land.

Healing the Environment

An incredible thing occurred in the seaside village of Rukua. The coral reef near this village had begun to die some years ago. Since their livelihood depended on the fish that fed off the coral reef, the villagers were becoming desperate. After they humbled themselves before God, their coral reef came back to life and the fish returned.[9] Think about that! It takes hundreds of years for a coral reef to grow. But God restored their coral reef literally overnight. Now the same thing has happened in another village, Nateleira.

In the village of Nuku, up in the interior of Naitasiri, the primary source of water had been polluted and acidic for more than forty years. Three days after the villagers' repentance, Nakauyaca says, "God healed the creek." It became clean and pure again.[10]

Fijians are telling similar stories all around the country. In some places, fish have returned to lifeless areas of the sea. In another place wild pigs were destroying the crops. They suddenly went away. As these stories have accumulated, chiefs and other leaders in the islands are inviting the Healing the Land team to their areas. In a number of places where they've ministered, the team has seen 100 percent of the people repent and declare their allegiance to Jesus Christ.

Rewriting the Scripts

The Word of God is not just affecting the interior, either. Vini Guanavinaka, a leader of YWAM's School of Biblical Counseling in Kona, says of her native Fiji, "There is an increased response to evangelism…and a new desire to integrate Christianity into everyday life." She said Indo-Fijians, mostly Hindus, are now coming to the Lord as well.

The number of believers has doubled. Revival is also bearing fruit on a personal level.[11]

In the business world, Fijian Kalara Vusoniwailala says, "In [the capital city of] Suva, almost every business has a Bible study going during the week. There is an awakening, and they want to understand the implications of their faith."[12]

Similarly, groups of professionals in the media meet regularly to delve into the Word, asking God how to conduct themselves in their industry. Vini tells of one prominent TV personality who rewrites the scripts to be sure the news presentation is fair.[13]

I don't think I've seen a more literal demonstration of 2 Chronicles 7:14 in my lifetime. We promised the Fijian delegates who came to seek our help to do everything in our power to help maximize what was going on. We will be giving more training in Fiji. Our goal is to help the people spread this transformation beyond their borders.

This kind of thing isn't just for Fiji. God promises every one of us, "If my people, who are called by my name, will humble themselves and pray and seek my face and turn from their wicked ways, then will I hear from heaven and will forgive their sin and will heal their land" (2 Chron. 7:14). I look forward to seeing what happens next. We'll see what God does in Fiji and in the nations where Fijians go as missionaries.

Chapter 31

Jesus,
the Living Word

Whatever we face, in whatever country, God has the answers. No matter how hardened or unbelieving or morally polluted or oppressed the nation, he wants to bring life and restoration. We need more than plans or strategies. As we've seen in the example of Fiji, it will take the power of the Holy Spirit along with the Word to bring healing.[1]

Jesus himself is the source of all life and healing. We need to know him through his Word, to see Jesus on every page. The Bible wasn't written like other books. It was written by people who had their minds supernaturally moved upon by the Holy Spirit.[2] It should be read in the same way. The more time you spend in the Word with the Spirit of God anointing your mind, the more you will discover Jesus throughout the Word of God.

The first chapter of John says, "In the beginning was the Word, and the Word was with God, and the Word was God.... and the Word became flesh, and dwelt among us."[3] We build on the right foundation for transforming people and nations when we understand who God is, as we love him and come to know his ways.

As a boy of seven, I memorized the names of all sixty-six books of the Bible. Many years later, a pastor friend in South Africa was telling me about a sermon he'd heard from Oral Roberts. The great healing evangelist claimed you could find Jesus in every book of the Bible. As soon as my friend said this, I started listing the books in my mind, thinking of immediate examples. Then I went deeper, searching in the Word. I'd encourage you to do the same. Look for Jesus in every book. Meanwhile, here's some of what I found.

Jesus throughout The Book

Jesus, the living Word, is the creator of Genesis, the liberator of Exodus, the high priest of Leviticus, the good spy of Numbers, the lawgiver of Deuteronomy, the conqueror of the book of Joshua, the righteous judge in Judges, and the kinsman-redeemer in the book of Ruth. Jesus is the second David in 1 and 2 Samuel, the King of kings in 1 and 2 Kings; and in 1 and 2 Chronicles, he's the record keeper. He is the rebuilder of the temple in Ezra. Jesus is the builder of our wall of protection in Nehemiah. He's the king who saves his people in Esther.

In Job, he is the Redeemer who lives, who releases double blessings after Satan has robbed us. He's the object of our praise and worship in the book of Psalms. He's the wisdom of Proverbs, the great preacher of Ecclesiastes, the lover of our souls in Song of Solomon.

Jesus is the king high and lifted up in Isaiah, and the government is on his shoulders; yet he's also the suffering servant who is beaten and dies for us. He's the weeping prophet of Jeremiah, brokenhearted over the sins of his people. He's the tears of God in Lamentations. In Ezekiel, the prophet falls motionless before Jesus, the one whose appearance is like burnished bronze. In Daniel, he is the fourth man in the fiery furnace and the stone not made by hand that destroys the foundations of the kingdoms of the world.

Jesus is the brokenhearted husband in the book of Hosea. He's the latter rain promised in Joel. He's the cascading justice flowing down from above in Amos. In Obadiah, he's the ruler and judge of the nations. He's the God of the second chance in the book of Jonah. He acts justly, loves mercy, and walks humbly with his God in Micah. In Nahum, he's the wrath of God. He writes the vision and makes it plain in Habakkuk, and we're promised that the knowledge of Jesus, the glory of God, will cover the earth as the waters cover the sea.

He sings over us with joy in Zephaniah. He's the latter glory of Haggai and the shaker of nations. In Zechariah, he's the one who cleanses the robe of the high priest and says to us, "It's not by might, nor by power, but by my spirit." In Malachi, Jesus brings the generations together, fathers to sons and sons to fathers.

In Matthew, he's the Messiah; in Mark, the Supreme Commander; in Luke, the Son of Man; and in John, the Son of God. He's the builder and the head of the church in Acts. He is the Second Adam who brings us to Abba Father in Romans, making it possible for us to be adopted as joint heirs with him. In 1 Corinthians Jesus is the love that is greater than faith and hope. In 2 Corinthians, he is the true apostle. He models all the fruit of the Spirit in Galatians; he's the one in whom there is neither Jew nor Greek, neither slave nor free, neither male nor female. We are one in him, the unifier of the Body.

Ephesians reveals Jesus as the chief cornerstone and the full armor of God that we put on: the helmet of salvation, the breastplate of righteousness, the truth around our loins, the gospel of peace on our feet, the shield of faith, and the sword of the Spirit. In Philippians, he's the one who emptied himself, leaving the glories of heaven, dying and going to the bottom of hell itself to be resurrected by his Father. He will be lifted above every name. Every knee will bow before him and confess that he is Lord, to the glory of the Father; and through Jesus Christ, we can do all things. In Colossians, we see that he created the world and is still holding everything together, including our lives, our families, and our ministries.

First Thessalonians shows Jesus caring for us as a nursing mother cares for her child and as a father cares for his children. Second Thessalonians reveals him as the returning King, coming in great glory and majesty. In 1 Timothy, he's the one mediator between God and man and the true model of eldership. Jesus reaches across generations again in 2 Timothy, uniting the faith of the grandmother Lois, the mother Eunice, and the son Timothy.

He's the purifier of the church in Titus and the one who frees the slaves in Philemon. In Hebrews, Jesus is the true rest of faith, the high priest after the order of Melchizedek, the author and finisher of our faith. He is the good works that accompany lively faith in James. In 1 Peter, during times of persecution and martyrdom, Jesus says to his people, "Cast your cares upon me for I care for you." He is precious in 2 Peter.

He says in 1 John that if we confess our sins, he will forgive us and cleanse us. If we know him, we'll love him and keep his commandments. In 2 John he's the perfect pastor who cares for his own, and in 3 John he's the pioneer leader who takes care of strangers who are pioneering, especially those with traveling ministries. In Jude, he warns of false prophets—those like Cain, who murdered his brother; Balaam, who cursed God's people; and Korah, who divided his brothers.

He's the glory, the majesty, dominion, and authority, before all time, now and forever. In the book of Revelation, Jesus reveals himself to John, who falls down like a dead man. It is too wonderful, too awesome, for John to see him in his glory. People from every nation, tribe, people group, and language group will honor and praise him with songs in their languages and dances from their cultures.

He's the One who rides the white horse and defeats the dragon and the beast. Every individual who ever lived will stand before him as he sits on the great white throne. He will judge everyone, separating the righteous from the unrighteous. Revelation 21 shows how the nations will come and lay their glory at his feet, the glory they learned through Jesus in the Word of God. And he is, as the final chapter says, the Alpha and Omega, the beginning and the end, who was and is and is to come, the Almighty. Jesus is the Word within the Word, made real by the Holy Spirit. He will become the Word within our lives, our societies, and every nation on earth.

Let's Do It!

As we study the Bible, we can learn God's ways. We see how he has led people in the past. This gives us a working model as we face modern-day struggles. The more we study his Word, the more we will discover answers, even for the biggest issues of our time.

Sometimes it seems the world's problems are unsolvable. How can anyone turn around a people with ingrained evil habits and bitter fruit?

God faced the same problem when he delivered his people from bondage in Egypt. After four hundred years, the Hebrews had a slave mentality. Though they experienced salvation and deliverance through the blood of Passover, they knew nothing about how to conduct themselves, their families, their social groupings, or their country.

God used Moses to disciple those millions of escaped slaves, to build them into a nation. In the following centuries that rather small tribe blessed the whole world, just as God promised Abraham they would. They did so by giving us the Bible and Jesus, God's Son. We can now take the Word and the Living Word to everyone who is still waiting. We can change the whole world. We can build and rebuild nations—those who have lost The Book for millennia, those who have recently discarded it, and those who've never had the opportunity to hear or see it at all.

Openness Is Coming!

In 1985, something unusual happened while I was speaking in Tuscula, Finland, at a national conference held in a large tent. All of a sudden, I began to know what God was about to do just east of us, in the Soviet Union. I told the Finns, "God is telling me that the Soviet Union is *opening*." Then I saw a picture of believers preaching freely on the streets of Russia. I saw Bibles being given out openly and Soviet missionaries going to every part of the globe. I shared all of this with the crowd in Finland as God was showing it to me. I remember well their reaction when I made that declaration. Their faces seemed to say, "Oh boy, listen to this crazy preacher!"

The very next year, in 1986, Gorbachev announced that *glasnost*, the Russian word for "openness," had come to the Soviet Union. Following the tragedy at Chernobyl, which exposed the depth of the government's deception, the Soviet Union began to open up. There were, of course, many other factors that led to the end of communist rule, too numerous to explain here. But as I watched events quickly unfold in Russia and Eastern Europe, I remembered how the Lord had spoken to me in the tent that evening in Tuscula, Finland. God said openness was coming. He wanted us to get ready.

Within a short time, I found myself preaching on the streets of Russia without interference, just as God had predicted. In fact, in one city where I preached in an open square, policemen came up to me, one at a time, quietly asking for Bibles.

Boris Yeltsin, the new leader of Russia at that time, asked the church to send 125 million Bibles so that every student could have a copy. Many mission groups got together in 1990 and sent in about 25 million Bibles. But we were not prepared to supply as many as the government requested. What a lost opportunity!

Now we are on the verge of another historic challenge.

We Must Get Ready

Years ago, Brother Andrew organized clandestine Bible distribution in China. Among other amazing accomplishments, his volunteers managed to get a million Bibles into China by barge from Hong Kong.[4] Later, businesspeople in Beijing challenged the Chinese government to allow Bibles to be printed. "Why are you afraid of the Bible?" they asked.

The government agreed to print Bibles. Some YWAMers became a part of the printing team. Each year since the program began, between one million and three million Bibles have been printed in China. With government approval, others have brought Bibles into China for distribution. So far there has been no serious opposition. Of course, China's population now stands at about 1.281 billion (1,281 million!). And with the number of believers growing by thousands every day, there still aren't nearly enough Bibles in China.

We mustn't squander another opportunity. We must get his Word out to the people. He is counting on us, eager to walk with us to carry his Word all over the earth. He wants us to prayerfully search the Scriptures for answers to every problem humanity is facing. He has placed this priceless treasure in our hands. It's time to use it.

A Parable for the Nations

I am grateful to Bob Moffitt for allowing me to include the following parable from his book *If Jesus Were Mayor*.[1] It sums up so much of the spirit of what I have tried to say in this book.

The Parable of Juan

Juan sensed a call of God to move to an unchurched area in his rapidly growing city and start a church. Actually, every time he rode a bus to and from work, the bus passed by the squatter community of Las Pavas. Juan felt a strange attraction to the people who lived there. He didn't have much training—just a few Bible school extension classes. What he did have was a passion to see people come to know Jesus.

Juan discussed it with his wife, and they decided to move to Las Pavas with their two young daughters. They rented a small, one-room wooden shack. Las Pavas had no water, no electricity, no school, and no health clinic. The roads were dirt. The people were poor. They lived in shacks made of tar paper, tin, old tires, cardboard, used boards, and anything else they could find for shelter. It was tough living, but Juan and his wife believed God had called them to live and minister there.

Juan worked during the day, but he used his evenings to visit neighbors and invite them to his home for Bible study. He devoted his weekends to being a pastor. Within a few months, a small group of women and children gathered each Sunday in Juan's one-room house. In a few more months, they were able to rent a room that served as a meeting place. Juan had about twenty women and numerous children in his congregation, but there were no men. The men in the community liked Juan but thought religion was something for women and children.

Juan was a faithful and loving pastor. He rose early every morning to pray for his people and to study the Bible. After the first year, there was good fellowship but not much growth. Juan and his wife found that the living conditions were weakening them physically. Their little daughters were often sick. Juan did not earn enough money to get them proper medical care. Juan was discouraged.

Early one morning, about four o'clock, Juan got up quietly. As usual, he was careful not to waken his wife and daughters. He had hung a plastic curtain to divide the room. At night, it separated the sleeping area from the living area, which was furnished with a table and four chairs. Juan sat at the table and lit the wick of an old milk can. It was full of paraffin and served as a lamp. He opened his Bible and began to read. This particular morning he was reading Isaiah 58. He read about God's concern for the hungry, for the naked, for the homeless, for the oppressed.

Juan's heart cried out silently: God, I see your concern for the poor in the Bible. Why don't I see it here in Las Pavas? Juan was deeply touched by the needs of the people, and a tear ran down his cheek as he prayed. As he was meditating on the difference between his experience and what he was reading, there was a soft knock at the door.

Immediately, Juan walked to the door, but he didn't open it. It was dangerous to open your door to a stranger in the dark. "Who is it?" Juan whispered.

A soft voice said, "I'm Jesus, Juan."

"Who are you really?"

The voice again said, "I'm Jesus, Juan."

The voice sounded so gentle that Juan almost believed it was Jesus. He quietly slid the locking bolt off the door and carefully opened it just a crack. He could see the silhouette of a man in the dark, and he did not look threatening. Juan opened the door a little wider and said, "Come in."

But Jesus said, "No, Juan, I heard your cry this morning. I came so you could show me the things that trouble you here in Las Pavas." Juan quickly and quietly stepped outside, a little surprised by his obedience to this invitation. He shut the door behind them.

Juan said, "Okay, Jesus, but stay close by me. This is the rainy season, and I know where to walk to miss the puddles."

"Okay, Juan," Jesus said. "I'll follow you."

They began their walk down the winding path. As they did, Juan said, "Jesus, over in that shack is a single mother. She sells her body—in her house and in front of her little children—to make money for food." They walked a little further. "And in that tar-paper shack is a family. The man is an alcoholic. He often comes home drunk and beats his wife and kids. The whole area can hear him yelling. Jesus, I can't stand it when I hear the screams, but there's nothing I can do."

They walked further and Juan said, "Hold your nose as we go by here. This is where everyone throws their garbage and uses the toilet." They could hear the rats scurrying among the trash. Then Juan pointed to another shelter. This one was larger than the rest. Juan said, "This, Jesus, is where the *presidente* of Las Pavas lives. He thinks he is a 'big' man. He collects money and tells the people it is to bring water and electricity here. But everyone knows he uses it for liquor and women."

Then Juan turned a corner, walked downhill, and began to circle back to where they had started. Juan pointed to a little shack at the bottom of the hill. "Jesus," he said, "this is one of the saddest things to me in all of Las Pavas. The woman who lives there was abandoned by the father of her three little children. They sleep on the floor. Whenever it rains, black water floods her little shack. Sometimes she sits up all night, holding the children so that they don't drown."

Juan heard someone softly weeping. He looked around. He could tell from Jesus' shaking shoulders that it was the Lord who was crying. Juan saw that the same things that broke his heart also broke the heart of Jesus. In a broken voice, Jesus turned and said, "Juan, I want to show you my intentions for Las Pavas."

Juan didn't know how it happened, but all of a sudden he and Jesus were looking down on Las Pavas. Juan could see the whole community. Jesus started talking about adequate housing. All of a sudden, the shacks turned into small, neat shelters. They weren't fancy, but they were nice. Jesus talked about jobs, and Juan could see the people of Las Pavas going to work. Somehow Juan could tell the jobs weren't high-paying. But he knew they paid enough to support the families of Las Pavas.

Jesus talked about water. All of a sudden there were standpipes appropriately spaced in the community, and everyone had clean water. Jesus talked about education and health. Right before Juan's eyes there was a school and a clinic. Jesus talked about beauty. Juan saw the garbage disappear. In its place children played in a field with trees and flowers. Jesus talked about healthy families where men and women and children respected and loved one another. Then Jesus talked about spiritual healing. Juan saw his little church full of families—including men. He was excited. He thought, *This is the kind of community I'd like.*

Of course, Jesus read his thoughts and said, "Juan, these are my intentions for Las Pavas. I want you to tell the people about my plans and begin to lead them there."

"But, Jesus," Juan protested, "I can't do that. How could my little congregation of women and children do anything? We are just struggling to survive."

"Juan, listen to me. I want you to share my plans with the people here, and then I want you to instruct your congregation to begin to serve the neighbors. Visit the sick. Visit the single mothers. Share with their neighbors. They can bring a cup of rice, a little soap, some sugar or salt, a few vegetables, and extra clothes to church on Sunday. Collect them in baskets and take them to those who are in greater need. They should do this every week. Then, you go and develop relationships with the city officials. Explore what is needed to bring water and power to Las Pavas."

"Jesus," Juan said, "we need to be realistic. These little things will never make a difference. I—"

"Juan, who created the world?"

"You did, Lord, but—"

"Juan, who divided the Red Sea so that the children of Israel could cross?"

"You did, Lord, but—"

"Juan, who fed the five thousand with five loaves and two fish?"

"You did, Lord, but—"

"Juan, I am the same yesterday, today, and forever. You do your part and I'll do the rest. Some things will not come to fulfillment until I return, but I want you to begin the process. You and your little flock are my ambassadors, my representatives. As you obey, I will begin to heal Las Pavas."

Juan was thinking about what Jesus said. Suddenly, he heard a rooster crow. He heard his wife beginning to stir behind the dividing curtain. He looked around. He was sitting at the table. The oil wick had gone out. It was becoming light outside.

Juan looked around for Jesus but saw no one. What happened? Juan thought, *Did I have a vision? Was it a dream?* Juan did not know. But he did know that Jesus had met him and that he had a new vision for the church and community of Las Pavas.

What if you were to walk through your community with Jesus? What if you were to talk to him about your ministry, your business, or your country? Would you hear his heart's desires, would you catch the sound of his weeping? Would you be willing to dare to do something that's impossible? Would you believe that the one who multiplied the loaves and fishes could multiply your efforts? Would you trust him to change your part of the world?

If we listen to him and do whatever he tells us, we will disciple entire nations. We will change the world. We will see his knowledge cover the earth, as the waters cover the sea.

Notes

All URLs have been accessed in recent months and are active web-sites to the best of our knowledge. With the passage of time, some web pages might be accessible only through a site's archives. In other cases, for example, where we've given only the home page, you might have to pay an entry fee to view a site's full range of pages.

Chapter 1—Losing and Finding The Book

1. See 2 Kings 21 and 2 Chron. 33.
2. 2 Chron. 33:4–5.
3. 2 Kings 23:7.
4. Winkie Pratney, *Devil Take the Youngest* (Lafayette, La.: Huntington House, 1985), 63–65.
5. 2 Chron. 33:6.
6. 2 Kings 21:16.
7. 2 Kings 21:23.
8. 2 Kings 22:2.
9. 2 Kings 22:8.
10. 2 Kings 23:2.
11. 2 Kings 23:4–6.
12. 2 Kings 23:25.

Chapter 2—What Will It Take?

1. World Christian Database, Center for the Study of Global Christianity, Gordon-Conwell Theological Seminary, www.worldchristiandatabase.org.

2. Ibid.
3. This is based on a ranking of nations by population as of July 2005, according to http://en.wikipedia.org/wiki/List_of_countries_by _population.
4. From interview with David Aikman by the author during a public gathering at the University of the Nations, Kona, Hawaii, May 25, 2006.
5. While the Chinese government continues to persecute members of the undocumented house churches, some government leaders are becoming secret believers, according to well-placed sources. They are like Nicodemus, who came to Jesus by night.
6. See Matt. 22:37–40 and Mark 12:28–31.
7. Americans for Divorce Reform, www.divorcereform.org/rates.html.
8. "US Prison Population Peaks," *BBC News U.K. Edition,* April 7, 2003, http://news.bbc.co.uk/1/hi/world/2925973.stm.
9. For statistics on drug use in the U.S., see National Institutes of Health, National Institute on Drug Abuse, www.nida.nih.gov /Infofax/nationtrends.html; see also www.nida.nih.gov/Infofacts /costs.html.

> For statistics on alcohol abuse in the U.S., see National Institutes of Health, National Institute on Alcohol Abuse and Alcoholism, www.niaaa.nih.gov/Resources/DatabaseResources /QuickFacts/default.htm. For economic consequences of alcohol abuse, see National Institutes of Health, National Institute on Alcohol Abuse and Alcoholism, *Updating Estimates of the Economic Costs of Alcohol Abuse in the United States: Estimates, Update Methods, and Data,* http://pubs.niaaa.nih.gov/publications /economic%2D2000/.

> For information on gambling abuse in the U.S., see *National Gambling Impact Study Commission Report,* "Problem and Pathological Gambling," North Carolina Family Policy Council, http://ncfamily.org/NGISC%20Final%20Report/4.pdf; see also The National Coalition Against Legalized Gambling, www.ncalg.org.

> For statistics on pornography use in the U.S., see Dick Thornburgh and Herbert S. Lin, *Youth, Pornography, and the Internet* (Washington D.C.: National Academy Press, 2002). Computer Science and Telecommunications Board, National Research Council, www.nap.edu/books/0309082749/html/R2.html; see also Protecting Children in Cyberspace, "Recent Statistics on Internet Dangers," www.protectkids.com/dangers/stats.htm; see also

Be Broken Ministries, "Statistics on Porn & Sex Addiction,"
www.bebroken.com/bbm/resources/articles/stats.shtml.

10. David B. Barrett, George T. Kurian, and Todd M. Johnson, *World Christian Encyclopedia*, 2nd ed., vol. 1 (New York: Oxford University Press, 2001), 772.

11. David B. Barrett, George T. Kurian, and Todd M. Johnson, *World Christian Encyclopedia*, 2nd ed., vol. 2 (New York: Oxford University Press, 2001), 224. Note that WCE uses the term *Great Commission Christians* (GCC) rather than numbering those who claim to be "born again" or "evangelical." GCC is defined on page 28, vol. 1 of WCE as "believers in Jesus Christ who are aware of the implications of Christ's Great Commission, who have accepted its personal challenge in their lives and ministries, are attempting to obey his commands and mandates, and who are seeking to influence the body of Christ to implement it."

12. The Barna Group, "Americans Are Most Likely to Base Truth on Feelings," February 12, 2002, www.barna.org/FlexPage.aspx?Page =BarnaUpdate&BarnaUpdateID=106, used by permission.

13. Ibid.

14. European Values Study, The Joint Information Systems Committee, www.jisc.ac.uk/coll_eurovaluesurveys.html.

15. Peter Ford, "What Place for God in Europe?" *Christian Science Monitor*, *USA Today*, February 22, 2005, www.usatoday.com/news /world/2005-02-21-god-europe_x.htm?POE=click-refer, August 3, 2006. According to Ford, whereas the European Values Study found that only 21 percent of Europeans thought religion was "very important," a similar Pew Forum poll found nearly three times as many Americans, 59 percent, who said their faith was "very important."

16. Brian C. Anderson, "Secular Europe, Religious America," *Public Interest*, Spring 2004, 143.

17. Patrick Johnstone and Jason Mandryk, *Operation World: 21st Century Edition* (Waynesboro, Ga.: Paternoster USA, 2001), 654.

18. Ibid., 651.

19. Noelle Knox, "Nordic Family Ties Don't Mean Tying the Knot," *USA Today World*, December 15, 2004, www.usatoday.com/news /world/2004-12-15-marriage_x.htm.

20. Johnstone and Mandryk, *Operation World*, 271.

21. Ibid., 270–71.

22. Ibid., 53, 271, 365–66, 651.

23. The Pew Forum on Religion and Public Life, "An Uncertain Road: Muslims and the Future of Europe," http://pewforum.org/docs /index.php?DocID=60.

24. Ibid.

Chapter 3—We Can Turn the Tide

1. Matt. 6:10.
2. Matt. 28:19–20.
3. Rom. 5:20.
4. Col. 1:16–17.
5. Col. 1:19–20.
6. John 20:21.
7. 1 John 4:4.
8. Col. 2:10.
9. "The light shines through the darkness, and the darkness can never extinguish it" (John 1:5, NLT).
10. John 8:12; Matt. 5:14.
11. Many know that YWAM launched a ministry called Mercy Ships in 1978. Not many know of another YWAM ministry called Marine Reach, started within YWAM by David Cowie in 1990. Marine Reach includes ships under 300 tons.
12. Isa. 9:2.
13. According to David B. Barrett, George T. Kurian, and Todd M. Johnson, *World Christian Encyclopedia,* 2nd ed., vol. 1 (New York: Oxford University Press, 2001), 849, "World A," defined as "unevangelized," numbered 1.6 billion or 26.9 percent in 2000.
14. Col. 1:12–14.
15. See Luke 10.
16. Matt. 13:33.
17. Lincoln College, University of Oxford, "John Wesley (1703–1791)," www.lincoln.ox.ac.uk/content/view/128/125/; see also Rejesus, The Story: Famous Followers, www.rejesus.co.uk/the_story/saint/saint4 /quotes.html.
18. Phil. 4:13.
19. Matt. 22:34–40.

Chapter 4—Revival or Transformation?

1. For more on the Welsh revival, see the Rev. Oliver W. Price, "The Welsh Revival of 1904–1905," Bible Prayer Fellowship, http://bpf.gospelcom.net//welsh.html.

2. For more on the Hebrides revival, see Duncan Campbell, *The Price and Power of Revival: Lessons from the Hebrides Awakening* (Fort Washington, Pa.: Christian Literature Crusade, out of print).

3. For more on the Pensacola revival, see *Religion and Ethics Newsweekly*, "Brownsville Assembly of God Church," June 2, 2000, www.pbs.org/wnet/religionandethics/week340/cover.html; see also Steve Beard, "Shake, Rattle, and Repent: The Pensacola Outpouring," www.goodnewsmag.org/library/articles/beard-ja96.htm, article originally published in *Good News*, July/August 1996.

4. Rom. 12:2.

5. Jeff Fountain, "Shapers of Our Modern Age," 2, 3, Hope for Europe, http://www.hfe.org/cms_images/docs/shapers.pdf.

6. Fountain, "Shapers," 3.

7. John Wesley, *The Journal of John Wesley* (Grand Rapids: Christian Classics Ethereal Library, 2000), www.ccel.org/ccel/wesley/journal.vi.ii.xvi.html?highlight=i,felt,my,heart,strangely,warmed#highlight.

8. Fountain, "Shapers," 9.

9. Ibid.

10. Ibid., 13.

11. Ibid., 9.

12. Ibid.

13. Ibid., 11.

14. Ibid.

15. Ibid., 12.

16. Ibid.

17. Ibid., 11.

18. Edward Coleson, "English Social Reform from Wesley to the Victorian Era," Wesley Center for Applied Theology, http://wesley.nnu.edu/wesleyan_theology/theojrnl/06-10/07-2.htm.

Chapter 6—A True Nation Builder: William Carey

1. Ruth and Vishal Mangalwadi, *The Legacy of William Carey: A Model for the Transformation of a Culture* (Wheaton, Ill.: Crossway, 1999).

2. Gen. 1 and 1 Tim. 4:4.

3. Ps. 145:10, KJV.

4. Gen.1:28.

5. Mangalwadi and Mangalwadi, *Legacy*, 22.

6. Vishal Mangalwadi, *Missionary Conspiracy: Letters to a Postmodern Hindu* (Mussoorie, India: Nivedit Good Books, 1996), and Vishal

Mangalwadi, *India: The Grand Experiment* (Farnham, U.K.: Pippa Rann, 1997).

7. Mangalwadi and Mangalwadi, *Legacy*, 72.
8. Ibid., 23.
9. NCDHR (National Campaign on Dalit Human Rights), www.dalits .org/default.htm.
10. For more information, see Barbara Crossette, "Caste May Be India's Moral Achilles' Heel," *New York Times*, October 20, 1996, Mount Holyoke College, www.mtholyoke.edu/acad/intrel/caste.htm; see also Eric Margolis, "India's Hidden Apartheid," *Sikh Spectrum*, November 2002, www.sikhspectrum.com/112002/eric_caste.htm; and Gopal Guru with Shiraz Sidhva, "India's 'Hidden Apartheid,'" *The Courier*, September 2001, www.unesco.org/courier/2001_09/uk /doss22.htm.
11. According to the Rev. Dr. J. N. Manokaran of Global Resources Development in Chennai, India, more than 300,000 Indian pastors, missionaries, and evangelists are bringing many thousands to Christ despite severe opposition in certain pockets of the country.
12. Patrick Johnstone and Jason Mandryk, *Operation World: 21st Century Edition* (Waynesboro, Ga.: Paternoster USA, 2001), 311.
13. Ibid., 6. Note that when in-country missionaries are counted, India may rank second in *total* number of missionaries sent, not the number sent per capita.

Chapter 7—A Man You Need to Meet: Abraham Kuyper

1. This chapter is summarized from Jeff Fountain's "Shapers of Our Modern Age," www.hfe.org/cms_images/docs/shapers.pdf, used by permission of the author.
2. Abraham Kuyper differentiated between spheres of authority, which he called "domains of sovereignty," such as family and government, and areas of influence, such as the arts. God gives some of his authority by making covenant with people—all authority spheres are a result of man's covenant with God or with one another. Israel was blessed because it was a covenant nation. Individuals who make a covenant with God bring blessings to their entire country.
3. *Vrije Universiteit*, www.english.vu.nl/about_the_VU/index.cfm. See History and Mission.
4. Fountain, "Shapers," 33–34.
5. See 2 Kings 20:12–19.

6. "Visual Faith: A Christian Recovery of the Arts, A Conversation with Dr. William Dyrness," *Cutting Edge* vol. 6, no.1 (Winter 2002), 9–11; also confirmed with personal letter from former student who was in the student assembly when the college president reported his response to the producer.

7. Luke 19:13, KJV.

Chapter 8—Skiing with Bibles: Hans Nielsen Hauge

1. The author gained much of his knowledge of Hans Nielsen Hauge from conversations with Alv Magnus, whose thesis is not yet available in English. The most comprehensive English source is Joseph M. Shaw, *Pulpit under the Sky: A Life of Hans Nielsen Hauge* (Minneapolis: Augsburg, 1955). Other sources include: Jeff Fountain's "Shapers of Our Modern Age," www.hfe.org/cms_images /docs/shapers.pdf; Winkie Pratney, "Hans Nielsen Hauge," *The New Testament Church Planting Digest* 2, no. 98 (June 4, 2002), www.world-missions.org/digests; "The Life of Hans Nielsen Hauge," *Augsburg Now* 60, no. 1 (Fall 1997), Augsburg College, http://www .augsburg.edu/now/archives/fall97/hauge.html; and *Lutheran Calendar* 29 March (1824), "Hans Nielsen Hauge, Renewer of the Church," Anglican Resource Collection, http://justus.anglican.org /resources/bio/index.html.

2. Pratney, "Hans Nielsen Hauge."

3. Shaw, *Pulpit*, 4.

4. Hauge quoted by Shaw, *Pulpit*, 162. *Pulpit* also includes the full text of two of Hauge's briefer writings, in which this quote appears, 221–34.

5. Fountain, "Shapers," 21.

6. Shaw, *Pulpit*, 74.

7. Ibid., 43.

8. Ibid., 10.

9. Exod. 20:5–6.

Chapter 9—An "Overnight" Success Story

1. Omniglot: A Guide to Written Language, s.v. "Korean," www.omniglot.com/writing/korean.htm.

2. Dr. H. Vinson Synan, "The Yoido Full Gospel Church," *Pentecostal-Charismatic Theological Inquiry International Cyberjournal for Pentecostal-Charismatic Research*, www.pctii.org/cyberj/cyberj2 /synan.html.

3. Ibid.

4. Reformed Online, "Information about the Republic of Korea," www.reformiert-online.net/weltweit/75_eng.php.

5. David B. Barrett, George T. Kurian, and Todd M. Johnson, *World Christian Encyclopedia*, 2nd ed. (New York: Oxford University Press, 2001), 682.

6. According to a June 20, 2000, article in the *Korea Herald*, www.koreaherald.co.kr, "The war left about 5 million people dead, wounded or missing, more than half of them civilians. It also left more than 10 million people separated from their families, 300,000 war widows and 100,000 war orphans;" see also Phil de Haan, "50 Years and Counting: The Impact of the Korean War on the People of the Peninsula," May 2002, Calvin College, www.calvin.edu/news /releases/2001_02/korea.htm.

7. Now Dr. Cho's church numbers 800,000, according to "Yoido Full Gospel Church," Wikipedia, http://en.wikipedia.org/wiki /Yoido_Full_Gospel_Church.

8. According to Central Intelligence Agency, *The 2005 World Factbook*, www.cia.gov/cia/publications/factbook/rankorder /2001rank.html, South Korea's ranking of sixteenth factors in its purchasing power parity (PPP), the measure most economists prefer when comparing living conditions from country to country. If you look just at nominal gross domestic product—the value of all final goods and services produced within a nation in a given year—South Korea ranks even higher, at number ten, according to "List of Countries by GDP (Nominal)," Wikipedia, http://en.wikipedia .org/wiki/List_of_countries_by_GDP_(nominal).

9. Patrick Johnstone and Jason Mandryk, *Operation World: 21st Century Edition* (Waynesboro, Ga: Paternoster USA, 2001), 388.

10. Norimitsu Onishi, "Korean Missionaries Carry Word to Hard Places," *Seoul Times*, October 19, 2005, www.theseoultimes.com /ST/db/read.php?idx=1193.

11. Ibid.

12. While the church is growing in India, the percentage of Christians is only 6 percent, according to World Christian Database, Center for the Study of Global Christianity, Gordon-Conwell Theological Seminary, www.worldchristiandatabase.org. As this figure grows, and as a critical mass of Indians applies the truths of God's Word, as has happened in South Korea, then we'll see India reach its potential.

13. Estimates vary. The World Christian Database, www.worldchristiandatabase.org, estimates that 41 percent of South Korea's population is Christian. Johnstone and Mandryk, *Operation World*, 387, estimates 31.67 percent.

14. Johnstone and Mandryk, *Operation World*, 388.

15. Former South Korean Presidents Noh (Roh) Tae Woo and Chun Doo Hwan were found guilty of treason, mutiny, and corruption. Noh (Roh) Tae Woo was sentenced to 22.5 years in prison, and Chun Doo Hwan was sentenced to death. On appeal the sentences were reduced to 17 years in prison and life imprisonment, respectively.

16. Learning Enrichment, "South Korea: Shaping a New Era," www.learningenrichment.org/wc_sou_three.html; see also John Borland and Michael Kanellos, "Broadband: South Korea Leads the Way," C-NET News.com, July 28, 2004, http://news.com.com /South+Korea+leads+the+way/2009-1034_3-5261393.html; and Joel Strauch, "Greetings from the Most Connected Place on Earth—South Korea: Where Broadband Is Cheap, and the Gaming Is Easy," *PC World*, February 21, 2005, http://www.pcworld.com /resource/article/0,aid,119741,pg,1,RSS,RSS,00.asp.

Chapter 10—Revolution in a Tiny Land

1. The story of Pitcairn summarizes the author's conversations with Professor Herbert Ford of Pacific Union College's Pitcairn Islands Study Center of California, interviews with the Pitcairners on the island in 1991, as well as information from *The Bounty* by Caroline Alexander (New York: Viking Penguin, 2003).

2. Alexander, *Bounty*, 355.

3. Ibid., 365.

4. Sir Charles Lucas, K.C.B., K.C.M.G., introduction to *The Pitcairn Island Register Book*, Society for Promoting Christian Knowledge (London, 1929), 15. *The Register* picks up its recordings of births, deaths, marriages, and remarkable family events on Pitcairn with the arrival of the *Bounty*, January 23, 1790, and continues through 1853.

5. Alexander, *Bounty*, 348.

6. From author's preface to *Bounty Trilogy*, Charles Nordhoff and James Norman Hall (Boston: Little, Brown, 1936), vii.

7. Alexander, *Bounty*, 354.

8. Recently, a court case focused unfavorable attention on Pitcairn, charging seven men under British law with having sex when they

were much younger with underage women. The alleged incidents happened up to forty-five years ago. According to the Pitcairn Islands Study Center, some Pitcairners have been convicted and are appealing their convictions before the Privy Council in England. The outcome of the appeal is not known at the time of this writing. Moral failure, if that is what happened, is always regrettable. See "British Foreign Office minister's rhetoric signals UK government plans to end habitation of Pitcairn says academic," Pacific Union College, Pitcairn Islands Study Center, http://library .puc.edu/pitcairn/news/releases/news31—08-20-03.shtml.

9. According to Professor Ford, after research done by Mrs. Pauline Ernst and the Connecticut Historical Society and others, experts believe that the Bible under glass on Pitcairn is the "Bounty Bible," and not the one once owned by Fletcher Christian. That Bible is now in the New York Public Library. The Bible that is on Pitcairn was the ship's Bible, used by Captain Bligh.

Chapter 11—The Greatest Revolution of All Time: Martin Luther

1. Paul Mizzi, "A Biography of the German Reformer, Martin Luther," *Truth for Today: Biblical Essays*, Trinity Evangelical Church, www.tecmalta.org/tft345.htm.
2. Ibid.
3. Ibid.; also Rom. 1:17, KJV.
4. Steven Kreis, The History Guide: Lectures on Early Modern European History, "Lecture 3: The Protestant Reformation," www.historyguide.org/earlymod/lecture3c.html; also *Encyclopedia Britannica Concise*, http://concise.britannica.com/ebc/article -9370750/Martin-Luther.
5. Mizzi, "A Biography."
6. Dr. Martin Luther, "Disputation of Doctor Martin Luther on the Power and Efficacy of Indulgences," 1517, http://www.iclnet.org /pub/resources/text/wittenberg/luther/ninetyfive.txt.
7. Mizzi, "A Biography."
8. Ibid.
9. See Exod. 19:5–6; 1 Pet. 2:9–10.
10. Mizzi, "A Biography."

Chapter 12—Unlocking the Wealth

1. "How Much Information?" School of Information Management and Systems, U.C. Berkeley, Oct 27, 2003, http://www2.sims

.berkeley.edu/research/projects/how-much-info-2003/; also, Bob Herbert, "Miracles at Warp Speed," *New York Times*, December 31, 1999, A 21.

2. Mariano Grondona, "A Cultural Typology of Economic Development," in *Culture Matters*, ed. Lawrence E. Harrison and Samuel P. Huntington (New York: Basic Books, 2000), 54–55.

Chapter 13—John Calvin and the Smelliest City in Europe

1. Much of this information comes from a message by Tom Bloomer during a walking tour of Geneva, Switzerland, in July of 1996. Jim Stier includes a chapter by Tom Bloomer, telling Geneva's amazing story, in his forthcoming book, *Transformation for the Nations*. Contact: contagem@jocum.org.br.

2. Col. 3:23.

3. Max Weber, *The Protestant Ethic and the Spirit of Capitalism* (New York: Scribner Library, 1958). Weber wrote, "We thus take as our starting-point in the investigation of the relationship between the old Protestant ethic and the spirit of capitalism the works of Calvin, of Calvinism, and the other Puritan sects" (89). Weber says this after quoting from Montesquieu (45), who said in his Esprit des Lois, Book XX, chapter 7, that the English "had progressed the farthest of all peoples of the world in three important things: in piety, in commerce, and in freedom." Weber goes on to say, "Is it not possible that their commercial superiority and their adaptation to free political institutions are connected in some way with that record of piety which Montesquieu ascribes to them?" (45). See also Charles W. Moore, "Socio-Economic Consequences of the Protestant Reformation," January 6, 1998, *Canadian Conservative Forum*, www.conservativeforum.org/EssaysForm.asp?ID=6062; Roger B. Hill, "History of Work Ethic," University of Georgia, College of Education, www.coe.uga.edu/~rhill/workethic/hist.htm; and Stanley L. Engerman, "Review of Max Weber's *The Protestant Ethic and the Spirit of Capitalism*," Economic History Services, March 1, 2000, http://eh.net/bookreviews/library/engerman.shtml.

Chapter 14—Laying Foundations for Freedom

1. "Henry Dunant," Wikipedia, http://en.wikipedia.org/wiki/Jean_Henri_Dunant.

2. 1 Cor. 15:6.

3. Acts 1:15.

Chapter 15—The Key: Who God Is

1. For more information about Francis Schaeffer, see "Francis Schaeffer," Wikipedia, http://en.wikipedia.org/wiki/Francis _Schaeffer.
2. Dr. Schaeffer spoke of implied truths as "presuppositional truths." A declared truth presupposes another more foundational idea—a presupposition. In other words, if you think about a declared truth carefully, you will come up with the idea that is its foundation. These four ideas are not explicitly stated in the first chapters of Genesis. They are presuppositional truths that are foundational to ideas clearly stated in these chapters.
3. C. S. Lewis, *Mere Christianity* (New York: Macmillan, 1952), 142.
4. Manu Tandon, "Indian Politics of Caste," December 21, 2005, *The World Forum*, www.theworldforum.org/story/2005/12/20/14636/189.

Chapter 16—Your Beliefs about God Matter

1. A "hierarchy" means that individuals are organized into ranks, each subordinate to the one above it.
2. See John 17; Phil. 2:9–10; Col. 1:13–20.
3. See John 5:18–24; Phil. 2:6–7.
4. Eph. 5:21; Mark 10:42–45.
5. Rev. 1:8.
6. "What Is Hinduism, and What Do Hindus Believe?" Got Questions.org, www.gotquestions.org/hinduism.html.
7. Acts 17:22–28.
8. 1 John 4:19.

Chapter 17—Key Truths about Us

1. Gen.1:27.
2. Ps.139:13–16.
3. John 11:35.
4. Isa. 55:9.
5. Gen. 3:15.
6. John 14:26; 1 John 2:27.
7. 1 Tim. 4:4.
8. 1 Cor. 2:9.
9. James 1:17.

Chapter 18—Truth Exists, and You Can Know It

1. See explanation of "presuppositional truths" in note 2, chapter 15.
2. Rom.1:19–20.

3. 2 Tim 3:16, NASB.

4. Ibid., NIV.

5. Matt. 24:35.

6. John 18:37.

7. Heb. 4:12.

8. Ps. 1:1–3; see also Ps. 119:97–105, 128.

9. The Barna Group, "Americans Are Most Likely to Base Truth on Feelings," February 12, 2002, www.barna.org/FlexPage.aspx?Page =BarnaUpdate&BarnaUpdateID=106, used by permission.

10. David B. Barrett and Todd M. Johnson, *World Christian Trends* (Pasadena, Calif.: William Carey Library, 2001), Global Diagram 34.

11. "The 2005 Transparency International Corruption Perceptions Index," Infoplease, http://www.infoplease.com/ipa/A0781359.html.

Chapter 19—We Are Responsible to Live According to the Truth

1. Jer. 21:8; Ezek. 33:11.

2. Luke 12:48; 2 Pet. 1:5–8.

3. Samuel Adams, *The Writings of Samuel Adams*, Harry Alonzo Cushing, ed. (New York: G. P. Putnam's Sons, 1905), 4:124, www.wallbuilders.com/resources/search/detail.php?ResourceID =20#25, item #11.

4. David Barton, "Unconfirmed Quotations," Wall Builders, www.wallbuilders.com/resources/search/detail.php?ResourceID=29.

5. John Eidsmoe, *Christianity and the Constitution* (Grand Rapids: Baker, 1987), 51, 53, quoted in *America's God and Country: Encyclopedia of Quotations*, William J. Federer (Coppell, Tex.: Fame Publishing, 1994), 48–49.

6. Daniel Webster, *The Works of Daniel Webster* (Boston: Little, Brown, 1853), 1:48.

7. Isa. 11:10–12; Rom. 11:3–5.

8. Judg. 7:7.

9. See Joshua 20.

10. Matt. 5:13.

Chapter 20—Why Nations Are Poor or Rich

1. Matt. 25:14–30.

Chapter 21—Japan: Partial Obedience, Partial Blessing

1. Michael Ireland, "Gallup Poll of Japan Finds Christianity on the Upswing," March 17, 2006, Assist News Service, www.assistnews .net/Stories/s06030105.htm. This Gallup Poll showed that belief in

Jesus is actually on the upswing in Japan, especially among the young.

2. Japan has the third largest economy in the world, after the United States and China, and the second largest market economy, measured on a purchasing power parity basis, with an estimated gross domestic product of $4.018 trillion in 2005, *The World Factbook,* https://www.cia.gov/cia/publications/factbook/geos/ja .html. Yet Japan's social ills are varied and sometimes extreme. Alcoholism is on the increase. A national survey conducted in 2001 by Japan's Health, Labor and Welfare Ministry estimated over two million alcoholics in Japan, according to "Japan Faces Growing Alcohol Problems," July 31, 2003, http://alcoholism.about.com /b/a/013857.htm. Japan ranks tenth in the world for suicides, according to "List of countries by suicide rate," Wikipedia, http://en.wikipedia.org/wiki/List_of_countries_by_suicide_rate. According to Michael Ireland, "Gallup Poll of Japan," a recent Gallup Poll in Japan found that 85 percent of Japanese teens often wondered why they exist (compared to 22 percent of American teens in a similar Gallup Poll.) Another disturbing trend is the *hikikomori*; as many as one million teens are committing this, a sort of "living suicide," locking themselves in their rooms and not coming out for years, according to Maggie Jones, "For Some in Japan, a Room Is Their World," *The New York Times*, January 15, 2006, *International Herald Tribune*, www.iht.com/bin/print_ipub .php?file=/articles/2006/01/13/news/shutins.php. Divorce, once rare in Japan, has more than doubled since 1975, according to Natalie Obiko Pearson, "More Japanese Untie the Knot," January 19, 2004, CBS News, www.cbsnews.com/stories/2004/01/19/world/main594084 .shtml. Domestic abuse wasn't acknowledged until very recently because of the shame, but a recent survey says 1 in 20 women fears for her life, according to Hiromi Ikeuchi, "Domestic Violence," Japanese Women Now, http://wom-jp.org/e/JWOMEN/dv.html. Avoidance of shame, called "loss of face," has also contributed to a general denial of mental illness until recently, even though Japan has the largest per capita number of hospitalized mental patients in the world, according to Hiroshi Matsubara, "In Japan, Psychiatric Care Still Mired in Dark Ages," *The Japan Times*, September 12, 2001, *World Health News*, Harvard School of Public Health, www.worldhealthnews.harvard.edu/gallery/mental.html; see also, Kazuko Hirota, "Better Services Needed for People with Mental

Illness: Message to Prime Minister of Japan, Junichiro Koizumi, the Mass Media, and the People of Japan," *Disability World* 12 (January-March 2002), www.disabilityworld.org/01-03_02/il/japan.shtml.

3. Matt. 13:33; Luke 17:21.
4. Clarence W. Hall, *Adventurers for God* (New York: Harper, 1959), 81–105. Hall personally visited Vories in Japan and observed his work. The information about Vories in this chapter is drawn from *Adventurers for God*.
5. Hall, *Adventurers*, 83.
6. Ibid., 90. The brotherhood lived on meager salaries but were able to draw on the treasury for emergencies.
7. Vories quoted in Hall, *Adventurers*, 90.
8. Ibid., 88.
9. Ibid., 92.
10. Ibid., 97.

Chapter 22—Japan's Extreme Makeover

1. *The Rising Son*, vol. 1 issue 2, The JapanNet, International Student Resource Ministry of Campus Crusade for Christ, www.thejapannet.com/prod01.htm.
2. Janet and Geoff Benge, *Douglas MacArthur: What Greater Honor* (Lynnwood, Wash.: Emerald Books, 2005), 170.
3. Ibid., 170–71.
4. Clarence W. Hall, *Adventurers for God* (New York: Harper, 1959), 100.
5. Ibid.

Chapter 23—Africa: Great Challenges, Great Hope

1. David B. Barrett, George T. Kurian, and Todd M. Johnson, *World Christian Encyclopedia*, 2nd ed., vol. 1 (New York: Oxford University Press, 2001), 13, lists percentage of African Christians as 9.2 percent in 1900; 45.9 percent in 2000.
2. The statistic of 69 percent Christian was derived by adding numbers of Christians in countries below the Sahara: Angola, Benin, Botswana, Burkina Faso, Cameroon, Congo Brazzaville, DR Congo (Zaire), Equatorial Guinea, Gabon, Guinea, Guinea-Bissau, Ivory Coast, Kenya, Lesotho, Liberia, Madagascar, Malawi, Mali, Mauritius, Mozambique, Namibia, Nigeria, São Tomé-Principe, Senegal, Seychelles, Sierra Leone, South Africa, Tanzania, Togo, Uganda, Zambia, and Zimbabwe, and dividing that figure by their

populations. Figures taken from Barrett, Kurian, and Johnson, *World Christian Encyclopedia*, 827–35.

3. Patrick Johnstone and Jason Mandryk, *Operation World: 21st Century Edition* (Waynesboro, Ga.: Paternoster USA, 2001), 21, 25.

4. The United Nations Human Development Index (HDI) rates countries according to poverty, life expectancy, illiteracy, and other indicators. Thirty of the lowest thirty-two countries on the HDI are in Africa, according to "Human Development Index," Wikipedia, http://en.wikipedia.org/wiki/Human_Development _Index. However, some countries were either unwilling or unable to be included on the HDI, including Afghanistan, Iraq, Liberia, North Korea, Serbia, Montenegro, and Somalia.

5. United Nations Department of Public Information, Strategic Communications Division, "Tragedy and Hope: Africa's Struggle against HIV/AIDS," *Africa Recovery*, August 2005, 3.

6. Joint United Nations Programme on HIV/AIDS (UNAIDS), *AIDS Epidemic Update 2004* and UNAIDS, www.unaids.org/en/Regions _Countries/Regions/SubSaharanAfrica.asp.

7. World Vision, "Bringing a New Perspective to the International AIDS Crisis," http://domino-201.worldvision.org/Worldvision /appeals.nsf/stable/hope_aidsindex_print2004.

8. The total of nearly 6 million dead comes from various BBC articles online. Sierra Leone: 50,000, http://news.bbc.co.uk/1/hi/world /africa/3865941.stm; Angola: 300,000, http://news.bbc.co.uk/1/hi /world/africa/countryprofiles/1063073.stm; Liberia: 200,000, http://news.bbc.co.uk/1/hi/world/africa/countryprofiles/1043500.stm; DR Congo: 3,000,000, http://news.bbc.co.uk/1/hi/world/africa /countryprofiles/1076399.stm; Sudan 1.5 million, and counting in continuing genocide, http://news.bbc.co.uk/1/hi/world /middle_east/countryprofiles/820864.stm

9. While government census puts the number of dead at 937,000, others expect this number will exceed one million as more exact figures emerge from the "Gacaca" war tribunals. Source: Reuters Foundation AlertNet, www.alertnet.org/thefacts/reliefresources /108117321274.htm.

10. Johnstone and Mandryk, *Operation World*, 24.

11. See Acts 15:19–20 for how open God is to those who turn from false religion to him.

12. These statements are based on research of only a few nations of Africa. The continent is overwhelmingly gifted with natural resources.

According to "S Africa and DR Congo Boost Ties," BBC News, January 14, 2004, http://news.bbc.co.uk/2/hi/africa/3393157.stm, one country alone, DR Congo has enormous deposits of gold, silver, diamonds, copper, cobalt, zinc, and uranium.

From Fred Bridgland, "The Pillage of Africa," *Sunday Herald*, June 5, 2005, www.sundayherald.com/50112, we learn that 90 percent of the world's known reserves of platinum are in South Africa and that oil resources in Africa may eventually match the Middle East.

There's gold in Madagascar, according to Camillo Premoli, International Mineral Resources, www.smedg.org.au/Premoli.htm.

Zimbabwe is rich with gold and boasts the world's second-largest platinum reserves, according to Abraham McLaughlin, "A Rising China Encounters US Clout in Africa," *Christian Science Monitor*, March 30, 2005, http://csmonitor.com/2005/0330 /p01s01-woaf.htm.

South Africa is responsible for 40 percent of all gold mined on earth so far. Another half-trillion dollars' worth is waiting to be mined there, according to University of Arizona, "Scientists Discover That 40 Percent of the World's Gold Is 3 Billion Years Old," *Science Daily*, September 16, 2002, www.sciencedaily.com /releases/2002/09/020916064654.htm.

Most of the world's gem-quality diamonds come from Africa (including South Africa, Botswana, Angola, Namibia, DR Congo (Zaire), Sierra Leone, Congo (Congo Brazzaville), and Siberia, according to Australian Museum Online, "Geoscience: The Earth," www.amonline.net.au/geoscience/earth/gem.htm.

From an article by Georges Nzongola-Ntalaja, "The Crisis in the Great Lakes Region," in *African Renaissance: The New Struggle*, ed. Malegapuru William Makgoba (Cape Town, So. Africa: Mafube Publishing Limited and Tafelberg Publishers Limited, 1999), 63–64, we learn that the Congo River has the greatest hydroelectric potential in the world. Part of this potential has already been harnessed through the Inga Dam. This hydroelectric complex has the potential of lighting up the whole continent of Africa, from Cairo to Cape Town. The same source says that with twelve months of rainfall in much of the rainforest and plenty of rain in the two savanna zones on each side of the equator, the Congo can also feed the entire continent. Today, it is estimated that less than 3 percent of its arable land is under cultivation.

13. Johnstone and Mandryk, *Operation World*, 21.

14. The Redeemed Christian Church of God, "Story of the Holy Ghost Congress," http://hgs.rccg.org/story%20of%20HG2.htm.
15. *Time*, February 7, 2005, 37–38.
16. George Kinoti, *Hope for Africa and What the Christian Can Do* (Nairobi, Kenya: African Institute for Scientific Research and Development [AISRED]), 1994.

Chapter 24—Latin America: Hope Delayed

1. Ruth Tucker, *From Jerusalem to Irian Jaya* (Grand Rapids: Zondervan, 1993), 57.
2. Daniel J. Boorstin, *The Discoverers: A History of Man's Search to Know His World and Himself* (New York: Random House, 1983), 257.
3. Ibid.
4. Thomas S. Giles, "How Did Native Americans Respond to Christianity? A Collection of Eyewitness Accounts," *Christian History*, Issue 35, vol. 11, no. 3, 1992: 20–23.
5. "The Canons and Decrees of the Council of Trent," in Philip Schaff, *Creeds of Christendom*, vol. 2, (Grand Rapids: Christian Classics Ethereal Library, 2002), 83.
6. Bartolomé de Las Casas, *Brief Account of the Destruction of the Indies*, quoted in Kay Stacy, "Las Casas, Man Who Made a Difference," http://historicaltextarchive.com/sections.php?op =viewarticle&artid=444.

Chapter 25—Winds of the Spirit in Latin America

1. For more on the Azusa Street revival, see Gary B. McGee, "William J. Seymour and the Azusa Street Revival," Assemblies of God USA, Enrichment Journal, www.ag.org/enrichmentjournal /199904/026_azusa.cfm.
2. As told to the author by Bráulia Ribeiro, YWAM President in Brazil, www.jocum.com.br.
3. Acts 2:41.
4. In 2000, Brazil had 17.2 million Assemblies of God followers in 113,300 locations, according to The Assemblies of God World Congress and 2000 Celebration, "World Report—Latin America/ Caribbean," http://2000.agcongress.org/cc/issues/000810/000810 _31_latinamcar.html. Note that this figure does not include the millions of Brazilians who belong to other Pentecostal denominations or attend a host of nondenominational charismatic churches or belong to the many noncharismatic evangelical churches.

5. David B. Barrett, George T. Kurian, and Todd M. Johnson, *World Christian Encyclopedia*, 2nd ed., vol. 1 (New York: Oxford University Press, 2001), Table 1-4.

6. Raul Ponce, trans. Cassie Acevedo, "El Tiempo," *Missions Frontiers*, April 2000.

7. Justin Long, "Least Reached Peoples," *Mission Frontiers* 28, no. 3 (2006), 8.

8. David Martin, *Tongues of Fire: The Explosion of Protestantism in Latin America* (Oxford, U.K.: Blackwell, 1990), ix.

9. Ibid., 92.

10. Greg Morsbach, "Chavez Deadline for US Preachers," BBC News, February 12, 2006, http://news.bbc.co.uk/2/hi/americas/4705740.stm.

Chapter 26—Set Your Sights on the World

1. 1 John 4:8.

2. Matt. 28:19–20.

3. The Latin root for the word *missionary* means "sent one."

4. Gen. 22:18.

5. Mark 16:15; Matt. 28:19–20; Acts 1:8.

6. Lisa Orvis, "Great Commission Catalyst," *Transformations*, vol. 1, 2004, 10.

7. Global Mapping International, http://www.gmi.org/.

8. For security reasons this data is available only to leaders of known missions organizations. For preliminary information, go to www.ywamconnect.com/sites/4k.

9. For up-to-date information, consult Wycliffe Bible Translators, www.wycliffe.org.

Chapter 28—On the Cutting Edge

1. Missions experts estimate there are between one billion and two billion active believers in the world. There are currently six billion people; to be conservative, take away one billion followers of Christ, and you have five billion to reach with Bibles. A conservative estimate would put five people per household, since developing countries have far more people per household. The cost per Bible for such distribution would vary widely, depending on the size of the language group and the corresponding print run. Some would cost as little as one dollar per Bible. But at the most expensive, if every Bible cost ten dollars, it would cost every believer only ten dollars to put a Bible in each of the one billion homes on earth without the gospel.

2. Bruce Wilkinson, *The Prayer of Jabez* (Sisters, Ore.: Multnomah, 2000), 89–90.
3. 1 Tim. 4:13.
4. "Pennsylvania Youth Group Holds Bible Reading Marathon," Assemblies of God News Service, October 2, 2002, http://ag.org/top/news/news_article_template.cfm?ArticleID =6601&NamedFormatID=2001Article&SearchDepartment =01-140&SearchBody=Ephrata&SearchStartDate=1/1 /1900&SearchMaxRows=6&SearchMaxRecordCount =1&SearchParameters=Ephrata&SearchType =TestForEachSearchTypeLabel.
5. Operation Mobilisation (OM), www.om.org.
6. Scripture Union International, www.su-international.org.
7. United Bible Societies, www.biblesociety.org.
8. Open Doors USA, P.O. Box 27001, Santa Ana, CA 92799, or www.opendoorsusa.org.
9. Paul Estabrooks, "Project Pearl Then and Nnow: What Is Its Impact on the Chinese Church?" ASSIST News Service, May 21, 2006, www.assistnews.net/Stories/s06050104.htm.
10. Strategic Resource Group, www.srginc.org.
11. "Christians Talk Faith in the Middle East with Innovative Internet Websites and Chat Rooms," ASSIST News Service, February 8, 2006, www.assistnews.net/Stories/s06020031.htm.
12. Ibid.
13. Ibid.

Chapter 29—Reaching the 7 Percent

1. A restricted access country is one where authorities make it illegal or very difficult to preach the Bible or make converts.
2. Luci Tumas, "Hearing the Christmas Story Again for the First Time," *In Other Words*, Wycliffe Bible Translators, November 2002, 9.
3. Current as of September 30, 2004, "History of Wycliffe Bible Translators," Wycliffe Bible Translators, www.wycliffe.org/history /wbt.htm.
4. Individual churches can contact SIL International for their Ethnologue: Languages of the World, to find a group they can adopt, at www.ethnologue.com.
5. To contact Bráulia Ribeiro, her website is www.jocum.com.br. Bráulia speaks fluent English, but the website is in Portuguese. You can contact her through the website or write to Bráulia Ribeiro, Caixa Postal 441, Porto Velho – RO, Brazil 78900-970.

6. For information on Global Recordings, formerly known as Gospel Recordings, go to http://globalrecordings.net/.

7. MegaVoice, www.megavoice.com.

8. David Barrett and Todd Johnson, *Our Globe and How to Reach It* (Birmingham, Ala: New Hope, 1990).

9. "Chronological Bible Storying," www.chronologicalbiblestorying.com.

10. "Following Jesus: Making Disciples of Oral Learners," www.fjseries .org.

11. From telephone conversation with Avery Willis, July 22, 2005. For more information on orality, or Chronological Bible Storying, go to www.chronologicalbiblestorying.com.

12. According to Dr. Sek Yen Kim-Cho, quoting UN sources.

13. See Dr. Sek Yen Kim-Cho's website, Sejong Studies Institute, www.sejongstudies.org.

14. See chapter 9.

15. See Sejong Studies Institute, www.sejongstudies.org.

16. According to Dr. Sek Yen Kim-Cho, quoting UN sources.

17. Matt. 19:26.

Chapter 30—The Spirit and the Word

1. 2 Cor. 3:6.

2. Luke 6:39.

3. Matt. 23:15–16.

4. John 4:24.

5. "Mutinies of Fiji Coup of 2000," Wikipedia, http://en.wikipedia.org /wiki/Fiji_coup_of_2000:Mutinies.

6. Some may wonder why Qarase was asking forgiveness for something he didn't do personally—the coup and violent acts against Indo-Fijians. He was following a biblical pattern demonstrated by Nehemiah (see Neh. 1:6–7) and Ezra (see Ezra 9:5–7). Even though you haven't personally done the sins committed by your nation or by your forefathers, you can ask God's forgiveness. This allows God to begin to heal your country.

7. *Let the Sea Resound*, DVD, directed by George Otis Jr. (Lynnwood, Wash.: The Sentinel Group, 2004).

8. George Otis Jr., "Pattern for Blessing," *Explorer Reports*, The Sentinel Group, http://sentinelgroup.org/explorer.asp.

9. *Let the Sea Resound.*

10. Otis, Jr., "Pattern for Blessing."

11. Lisa Orvis, "Fiji," *Transformations* (Kona, Hawaii: University of the Nations), October 2003, 8.

12. Orvis, "Fiji," 9.
13. Ibid.

Chapter 31—Jesus, the Living Word

1. Zech. 4:6.
2. 2 Tim. 3:16; 2 Pet. 1:20–21.
3. John 1:1, 14, NASB.
4. See chapter 28.

The Parable of Juan

1. Bob Moffitt, *If Jesus Were Mayor: Biblical and Historical Roots of Cultural Transformation Through the Church* (Phoenix, Ariz.: Harvest Foundation, 2005), 4–6.

About the Author

Loren Cunningham is the founder of Youth With A Mission (YWAM), a missions organization with nearly twenty thousand full-time staff from more than 150 nationalities and a wide variety of denominations. Loren has ministered in every sovereign nation and dependent country in the world as well as in scores of territories and islands. *The Book That Transforms Nations* draws on a lifetime of observing the nations as they change and a lifelong pursuit of hearing God's word for the nations. Loren and his wife, Darlene, live in Kona, Hawaii. Together, they serve in leadership capacities in YWAM and YWAM's University of the Nations. They have two grown children and three grandchildren. Loren is the author of four other books, *Is That Really You, God?*, *Making Jesus Lord*, *Daring to Live on the Edge*, and *Why Not Women? A Fresh Look at Scripture on Women in Missions, Ministry, and Leadership*.

Other Books by Loren Cunningham

WHY NOT WOMEN?
A Fresh Look at Scripture on Women in Missions, Ministry, and Leadership

by Loren Cunningham and David Joel Hamilton, $15.99

Why Not Women? brings light, not just more heat, to the church's crucial debate with a detailed study of women in Scripture; historical and current global perspectives; an examination of the fruit of women in public ministry; and a hard-hitting revelation of what's at stake for women, men, the Body of Christ, God's Kingdom, and the unreached. (ISBN 1-57658-183-7)

IS THAT REALLY YOU, GOD?
Hearing the Voice of God

by Loren Cunningham, $9.99

This practical guide to hearing God's voice shows how an ordinary man who was committed to hearing God and obeying Him became the founder of the largest interdenominational missions organization in the world. (ISBN 1-57658-244-2)

MAKING JESUS LORD
The Dynamic Power of Laying Down Your Rights

by Loren Cunningham, $9.99

We live in a world in which the protection and exaltation of individual rights has become an obsession. As Christians we believe that personal rights do hold great value. As a result, we can perform no greater act of faith and worship than to lay down these rights at the feet of the One who has gone before us, Jesus Himself! Loren Cunningham details proven steps to a transformed life of freedom, joy, and intimate fellowship with God. Includes study guide. (ISBN 1-57658-012-1)

DARING TO LIVE ON THE EDGE
The Adventure of Faith and Finances

by Loren Cunningham, $9.99

Living by faith is not the domain of only those Christians called to "full-time" ministry. What is important is not our vocation, but whether we are committed to obeying God's will in our lives. If we are willing to step out in faith, doing whatever God has asked us to do, we will see His provision. A Christian who has experienced this is spoiled for the ordinary. (ISBN 0-927545-06-3)

Other Books from YWAM Publishing

DISCIPLING NATIONS
The Power of Truth to Transform Cultures, 2nd Edition
by Darrow Miller, $15.99
The power of the gospel to transform individual lives has been clearly evident throughout New Testament history. But what of the darkness and poverty that enslave entire cultures? In *Discipling Nations*, Darrow Miller builds a powerful and convincing thesis that God's truth not only breaks the spiritual bonds of sin and death but can free whole societies from deception and poverty. Excellent study of worldviews. Includes study guide. (ISBN 1-57658-248-5)

THE WORLDVIEW OF THE KINGDOM OF GOD
by Scott D. Allen, Darrow L. Miller, and Bob Moffitt, $8.99
Today there are more churches and more Christians in the world than at any time in history. But to what end? Poverty and corruption thrive in developing countries that have been evangelized. Moral and spiritual poverty reign in the "Christian" West. Why? Because believers don't have the "mind of Christ." This Bible study explores the biblical worldview—the worldview of the kingdom of God—and why living it out is essential to leading a fruitful, abundant life. (1-57658-351-1)

GOD'S UNSHAKABLE KINGDOM
by Scott D. Allen, Darrow L. Miller, and Bob Moffitt, $8.99
The concept of the kingdom of God is one of the most confusing and misunderstood ideas in the Bible. Yet it's indisputable that the kingdom of God was the central theme of the teachings of Jesus. This profound Bible study explores God's kingdom, helping believers build a biblical understanding of the vision for which Jesus lived and died—a vision that transforms individuals and whole nations. (1-57658-346-5)

GOD'S REMARKABLE PLAN FOR THE NATIONS
by Scott D. Allen, Darrow L. Miller, and Bob Moffitt, $8.99
This Bible study shows that while God's redemptive plan plan begins with individuals, it's more comprehensive—more wonderful—than this. God's redemptive interest extends to the transformation of entire nations and cultures, encompassing every sphere of society. To be faithful to Jesus' command to make disciples of all nations according to the fullness of what Jesus intended, we must regain a comprehensive understanding of God's remarkable plan for the nations. (1-57658-352-X)

(continued on next page)

BUSINESS AS MISSION
The Power of Business in the Kingdom of God
by Michael R. Baer, $12.99

We are living in the Business Age. Like never before, Christian business leaders have the chance to play a pivotal role in transforming society and spreading the gospel. But seizing this opportunity requires thinking differently about God, about his kingdom, about his purposes in the world, and about business. Baer guides business leaders in developing the vital characteristics of a kingdom business—the kind of business that will free them to live fully integrated lives and lead organizations that significantly impact the world (ISBN 1-57658-388-0)

SPIRITUAL WARFARE FOR EVERY CHRISTIAN
How to Live in Victory and Retake the Land
by Dean Sherman, $12.99

God has called Christians to overcome the world and drive back the forces of evil at work within it. Spiritual warfare isn't just casting out demons; it's Spirit-controlled thinking and attitudes. Dean delivers a both-feet-planted-on-the-ground approach to the unseen world. With study guide. (ISBN 0-927545-05-5)

THE LEADERSHIP PARADOX
A Challenge to Servant Leadership in a Power Hungry World
by Denny Gunderson, $11.99

What is the key to effective leadership? The ability to organize and take charge? The ability to preach and teach? Entrepreneurial skill? A charismatic personality? According to Jesus, none of the above. Through the eyes of people who experienced Jesus firsthand, we discover insights that will challenge us to re-think our leadership stereotypes. Includes study guide. (ISBN 1-57658-379-1)

A BEAUTIFUL WAY
An Invitation to a Jesus-Centered Life
by Dan Baumann, $11.99

Center your life on Jesus and your choices will reflect his priorities. Learn to trust in him as you encounter fears. Spend time listening to his voice and walk in obedience to it. As your life becomes consumed with Jesus, let his life and love flow through you to the people around you. If you do this, you will see God's kingdom come here on earth as it is in heaven. (1-57658-312-0)

Call 1-800-922-2143 for a full catalog,
or visit our website at www.ywampublishing.com